BACK OF BEYOND:
A Memoir from the North Woods
By Susanne Kobe Schuler

This by far is the very best place. memories are to be cherished and shared. Remember – Enjoy!

Susanne Schuler

Cloquet River Press

ISBN: 978-0-9792175-0-0
Library of Congress Control Number: 2006940616

Published by: Cloquet River Press
                                  5353 Knudsen Road
                                  Duluth, MN 55803
                                  (218) 721-3213
Email the Publisher at: cloquetriverpress@yahoo.com
Visit the Publisher's website at:
                                  www.cloquetriverpress.com
Edited by Mark Munger
Cover Art and Design by René Munger

For sojourners, creators and memory-makers everywhere; for my parents Marie and Jack Kobe, and my sister Barbara Jean, who shared the journey.

Back of Beyond

A Memoir from the North Woods
By Susanne Kobe Schuler

Stories from the Lake Superior Basin
www.cloquetriverpress.com

TABLE OF CONTENTS

Why Wilderness? Ask men who have known it and who have made it part of their lives. They might not be able to explain but your very question will kindle a light in eyes that have reflected the campfires of a continent, eyes that have known the glory of dawns and sunsets and nights under the stars. Wilderness to them is real, and this they know: When the pressure becomes more than they can stand, somewhere back of beyond, where roads and steel and towns are still forgotten, they will find release.

Sigurd Olson
Ely, Minnesota

ONE:
THE JOURNEY BEGINS

Anna Marie, eight years old, dressed in a white T-shirt and faded denim bib overalls rolled up to her knees, stood in the middle of the cabin. Her short brown hair was cut Dutch Boy style; bangs and shingled in the back. She slowly brushed one leg against the other attempting to rub out irritating mosquito bites. Quick of movement and always chattering, for once Anna Marie was speechless. Wide-eyed, she surveyed the cardboard boxes and confusion surrounding her.

The cabin was cool and dimly lit from a single kerosene lamp. The feeble light cast finger-like yellow shadows around the newly built three-room cabin. Anna Marie was short. She attempted to reach for new dishes in the cupboards. She finally succeeded. The cabin smelled of fresh lumber, newly stained pine paneling and supper warming on the Heatrola.

She was cold, chilled as it was early spring. Cold too, from the excitement of this special day. This was all so strange, 1940, so long ago, yet so near when held close to her heart. A dream, a lifelong plan had slowly unfolded on the shore of beautiful Bear Island Lake near Ely, Minnesota. Many years of searching for the perfect spot for a small family resort finally had become a reality.

Supper ready, Anna Marie, her older sister Jean and their mother sat down to eat. The new silverware gleamed. So special to be the first ones to use it. Four small empty nail kegs propped up the table, which was still enclosed in a large uncrated cardboard box. The Skelgas cooking stove would be hooked up the following week. The simple food, hot dogs and beans seemed like a feast even though they were lukewarm.

No one said much during supper; each quiet with her own thoughts. Mother was concerned that all the curtains would get hung, cabins cleaned and the many chores done before the resort opened. One of the chores that caused Mother special concern was the installation of the Kohler light plant. The electricians had told her they needed more time. Would they be done before the June seventh opening? Jean wondered what it would be like to spend an entire summer away from her Duluth friends. Anna Marie was scared but excited. Would there be wild animals in the woods to hear and maybe see? Who would she play with? Could she bring toys from home and which ones?

Mother, Anna Marie and Jean were tired from the long trip; one hundred miles north from Duluth. The Chevrolet car, Rosie, had been packed to the ceiling. Father would join them on the weekend. His job as a traveling coal salesman occupied his week. The awesome task of untangling lumber leftovers from useable salvage awaited him on the weekends. There were small scraps of sawed lumber, a few piles of longer boards, green roof shingles and lots of fresh sawdust. All this needed to be sorted, moved and the area around each cabin raked.

Anna Marie liked walking barefoot through the new sawdust, especially if her feet were wet. The pale gold sawdust clung to her wet feet and packed between her toes. When she stamped her feet the sawdust flew in all directions.

Outside and across the calm, blue gray lake an orange-red sun was setting. Strange to really see a sunset, to watch it slowly slip behind the banks of clouds leaving a rich multicolored afterglow and silence-silence interrupted by frogs singing to each other along the shore. Waves quietly lapped against the shoreline.

Mother quickly extinguished the kerosene lamp and they crawled into bed, the new sheets cool against their tired bodies. Slowly the dark night sky crept over the resort. Anna Marie nestled closer to her big sister. Outside there were strange night noises, twitterings and mutterings of forest creatures as they settled down for the night.

Colonel, Jean's Boston terrier bulldog positioned himself as guard and protector by the front door. He sighed and rested his head on his paws, eyes half open yet alert. Finally, all was quiet as the adventure, the Journey Back of Beyond, began.

TWO:
PADDLING PARTNERS

In June of 1924, a log canoe rack rested against the side of a two-story frame house in the small town of Aurora, Minnesota. Tied securely to the rack with a chain and a padlock was a well-used Old Towne canoe. Inside the modest white house a young couple was busy packing heavy khaki colored canvas duffel bags and checking supplies off a long list. *Wooden matches. Mosquito dope. Fishing hat...*

"Hey, what's this book? Come on Marie, we can't be lugging extra stuff. It adds to the weight over portages. I know you. If you take one book, there'll be six more," laughed Jack, a groom of two weeks.

"It's only your book of Jack London poems. Thought we could read it at night by the campfire, kind of get into the spirit of the North Country," the woman, a new bride replied.

It was the middle of June. Two weeks earlier, Jack, in a dark suit, and Marie in a black taffeta dress, had been married at St. Andrews-By-The-Lake a tiny Episcopal church in Duluth. When asked why a black dress Marie's answer was that "it's the very best I own".

The groom had been four years old when he and his mother, Anna Barbara arrived in New York Harbor from Yugoslavia. When they landed, John (Jack as he was later called) was dressed in his best wool suit. His mother was weak, recovering from seasickness. The father and husband, John Matthew had ventured first to America to settle in Montana as a cook at a copper mine site, moving later on to the iron range of Northern Minnesota as a blacksmith.

The bride, Erma Marie, but always called Marie, was born in Nebraska and grew up in Oak Park, Illinois. For her, it had been a time of piano lessons, visiting relatives in Iowa, a cross-country trip by rail out west and excursions into Chicago to hear her parents play with the Chicago symphony orchestra. Her father taught her to drive their electric car. Summers were spent north, near Mercer, Wisconsin at a renovated lumber camp. These summers were shared with other families, relatives and her pet black and white collie, Prince. It was here that Marie began to love the woods, a love that would nurture and sustain her all her life.

While Marie was busy practicing the piano in Illinois, Jack was learning to be a northern woodsman, to handle and ax, paddle a canoe, use a compass and build a campfire. He was the oldest of six children. One chore he despised was picking blueberries. The family lived in Bangor location in rural Biwabik, Minnesota. A location was a housing development near iron ore mines for the miners and their families. Jack commuted from Bangor location to his job in Aurora, about seven miles. In winter, he used his two sled dogs, Snyder and Trixie, and in summer, a horse. The winter commute to Aurora was made in the dark, both early in the morning and returning in late afternoon. Sometimes Jack would hear wolves howling in the dark, causing him to hurry home. It was a lonely trail for a young man. In summertime, he tied his horse up with the mine mules. His job was timekeeper, later, bookkeeper at the Miller Mine.

After college, Marie accepted a kindergarten teaching position in Ironwood, Michigan. Years later she would laugh that there was a mysterious call to head northwest from Michigan to teach in Aurora, Minnesota at the Johnson School. The call was an excellent salary and an adventure.

Aurora in the early 1920's was a mining town with wooden sidewalks, dirt roads and an occasional loose cow wandering the town streets. Unmarried female teachers lived together in a boarding house with strict rules. Marie was engaged to a "city slicker"- a "Chicago fellow who didn't know a birch tree wasn't a pine"- when she moved to the little mining town.

One day female teachers were invited to tour the Miller Mine. Jack was the tour guide. And so, a dapper, dark brown haired, blue-eyed young man with a marvelous sense of humor met a serious, brown-eyed, adventurous, auburn haired young lady. The sparks flew! But the attraction was complicated by serious questions: How to break the young woman's engagement and how to deal with Marie's ailing mother in Oak Park? In time, both matters were resolved and Jack and Marie were free to fall in love.

Jack and his friends owned a cabin on Wynne Lake near Biwabik. It was reached by canoe or boat in the summer and skis in the winter. Sunday afternoons in the winter, young couples bundled up to cross country ski to the cabin, build a fire, cook supper and then ski back across the lake to their parked cars. There were no ski clothes for women back then so Marie had a local tailor make her a pair of ski trousers. It was difficult skiing with a calf length heavy wool skirt flapping around her calves but pants on a woman? God forbid! School officials called Marie on the carpet for her choice of clothing but she stood her ground.

Once in a while Marie was asked to play piano for silent movies showing in the local theater. This was a challenge, trying to keep up with the flickering black and white movie with appropriate music.

After their marriage there were many canoe trips to Crane Lake, to Lac Le Croix and other border country lakes of northern Minnesota. Most canoe trips were in June when the mosquitoes were the worst. A canoe trip in August might find you trying to paddle streams and rivers where the water was low. When possible, short canoe trips were taken on weekends, longer trips during vacation. On one canoe trip, they came upon a summer Indian camp. That evening, Jack and Marie were invited to powwow and dance around the campfire. It was special, very unique.

The years went by. The Old Towne canoe rested against the house waiting for Jack to hoist it on top of the car and head for a river or a lake. From this time, the couple took photographs, saved in old albums, black and white portraits of sunsets, beautiful lakeshore settings and campsites. In all of these pictures, Jack and Marie are grinning. Then the young couple moved to Wadena, Minnesota. Jack became a traveling coal salesman for northern Minnesota, a job he held for over thirty years. A daughter, Barbara Jean, named after Jack's mother, was born. Four years later, another daughter arrived. Life changed. And how!

Canoe trips were planned around when the relatives could baby sit. There was absolutely no way the couple would hang up their paddles and store their canoe. So Jack's sisters, brothers, some married, some single, baby-sat the two little girls. Sometimes the grandparents pitched in. It was family time, a time of sharing, of fun, of laughter. A time to sit around Grandma Ann's and Grandpa John's kitchen table feasting on grandma's homemade bread and sipping grandpa's home brew. That's the way it was done; family helping each other.

When Anna Marie, the youngest daughter, was three, the family spent several weeks with other relatives at a camp on Lake One near Ely. The camp, a primitive resort had no electricity or running water. Marie insisted on hauling an ironing board on top of the car. It later had t be tied to a canoe and brought to the camp. There were no roads to Lake One, Two, Three or Four. Sad irons for the ironing board had to be heated on the camp's wood cook stove.

The family moved to Iowa to Minneapolis to Duluth and then back to Minneapolis. Jack finally said "enough". He missed the cool lakes and green forests of northern Minnesota. And so, in the late 1930's, they settled for good in Duluth.

Jack and Marie always yearned to own woods property: Property on a lake where it was quiet, away from people, where the air smelled like pine and you could sit on a rock and watch the sun set. The place they found would have to have high ground, birch trees and, if possible, the call of loons to add their eerie songs to the wilderness silence.

While friends and relatives took over as caretakers of the two young girls, Jack and Marie's search began. Anna Marie learned to walk in Auntie Kay's house in Ely while her parents were out tramping in the bush. The seeking, the finding of just the right property consumed their leisure time. Sometimes they used the Old Towne for their explorations. Other times they traveled by car or boat. The search continued until Jack heard about a piece of property near Ely. The canoe paddles were tucked in the rafters of the garage and the canoe was turned upside down on its rack. The paddling partners had found their place in the woods and were about to become landowners.

THREE:
FACING WEST

"Stand back! Watch those sparks. Don't get too close. OK Steve, throw those logs on top. The kids will get the branches."

Father was calling to his brother Steve a short distance away. Father also kept his eye on his two daughters and their cousins. What a crew! Dressed warmly in woolen snowsuits, boots, mittens; the men wearing much the same clothing that they wore deer hunting. It was early spring 1940 and clouds of blue-gray wood smoke rose from three huge brush fires. There were uncles, friends, Mother and cousins all busy either chopping down brush with brush hooks or hauling twisted branches and short logs to the burning piles. There was a sense of urgency as June was only a few months away. Then the dream of a lifetime would become a reality.

Anna Marie stood back from the noisy group and watched hot flames consume the brush. It surely was exciting; men hollering, trees falling as axes smacked against tree trunks, cousins running, laughing and Mother pleading with the kids to keep hauling brush. A road to the resort was being built. Later, truck loads of gravel would be dumped, spread, and smoothed out. A rutted, overgrown, primitive and narrow road led from the highway to the lakeshore. Part of this road would be abandoned and another road built across the top of the hill. This road connected the cabins and wound gently down a short hill to the lake.

Mother leaned on a rake and looked toward the water. A small smile turned the corners of her mouth up. Her brown eyes glistened. She seemed lost in her thoughts. Anna Marie watched her wondering if she was getting sick or about to cry. There were tears in Mother's eyes.

The smoke, that's it; all this wood smoke from the fires, thought Anna Marie.

Mother brushed her eyes against the sleeve of her dark maroon wool jacket.

"Anna Marie, there's a bag of potatoes in the car. They're all scrubbed and ready for the fire. Find a spot where there are coals and just put them in. Should be baked in an hour or so. Be careful by the fire. Have Jean help you. I'll be down the way, by the road. There's brush to haul so hurry along. We need your help," Mother said talking as she walked away.

And so it came to be that two woods lovers became owners of 167 acres of prime lakeshore property on Bear Island Lake. This land was purchased for $1,000.00 on a contract for deed on January 20, 1940 and paid for by April 4th. The land was from the estate of Mary Kajanus. The long search was over! A search that began when Jack and Marie were newlyweds, and then young parents. The search took them all over northeastern Minnesota and even up the Gunflint Trail with a week's stay at Tuscarora Lodge where they realized that the Gunflint was too far from their home base of Duluth. The land for building a small family resort needed to be close to Duluth but far enough away to be a truly north woods retreat. Father could commute to the resort on weekends and his vacations. The family would be there from the time school let out in the spring until early fall just before school re-opened. Mother, the girls and hired help would run the resort. Mother was asked many times why a resort, why not just a cabin? Her reply was: "Too lonely. More fun to have people around. We'll keep it small, won't serve food, only housekeeping cabins." How many cabins? How big? Do we need a lodge? What shall we call the resort? And on and on.

Bear Island is located south of Ely about 12 miles down the road on Highway 21. Perfect, near a bustling town, in the Superior National Forest yet close enough to shops and supplies. The cabins were to be housekeeping cabins, complete in every way except for running water. A light plant would provide electricity. There was an artesian spring down near the dock where the well was sunk. Water would have to be hauled to the cabins in new galvanized steel buckets. R.E.A. (Rural Electrification Association) was years away from reaching Bear Island so there would be no indoor plumbing or running water until the power lines crept down Highway 21 in the late 1950's.

A total of four cabins were built. Three of them had two bedrooms plus a sitting room-kitchen area. One cabin, small, one-room, was called the honeymoon cabin. There was an ice house, a fish cleaning house, a small two room unfinished building called the store, five outhouses, a storage shed for the light plant and tools and a long dock. That was it: small, neat and manageable. Mother and Father insisted that the cabin interiors be pine-paneled and have casement windows that opened inward. Finnish carpenters, the very best Father could find, put up the pine paneling and built the kitchen cupboards. "No wood butchers allowed!" Father said. Mother chose a warm brown stain for the paneling and the exterior was stained a darker brown. Window trim was a soft cream color; roofs were shingled in a dark green to blend in with the tree tops. All cabins were 500 feet or more apart and close to the lakeshore but high enough and far enough back to catch the breezes blowing from the west across the bay.

There were fish in Bear Island Lake, lots of them. Walleyes, perch, northern pike, crappies, and rock bass. They were hungry too! The water was soft and clean. Inlet and outlet rivers kept the water moving plus springs bubbled up from the lake's bottom. The resort had a natural sandy beach with a gradual slope and no drop offs. At the end of the property was a natural sand bar at least two city blocks long. Mother was especially pleased that her favorite trees, the white birch, called by some the "lady of the forest", were plentiful. There were also poplar and pines. Over the years seedlings were planted each spring to replace dead trees. This was a job Anna Marie hated.

A name. What to call the resort? Should it be a hard-to-pronounce Indian name, a cutesy name or what? "Back of Beyond" was suggested. This name was Anna Marie's favorite; sort of mysterious, haunting and puzzling. Nope. Mother won and chose Buena Vista, loosely translated as "Good View".

Mother spent hours, days and weeks thinking about and purchasing furnishings for the resort. A trip to Faribault, Minnesota was made to purchase blankets from a woolen mill. The blankets were green wool with darker green pine trees just below the top binding. Bedspreads of beige and red nubby fabric were purchased from Sears in Ely. Mother sewed all the curtains, beige with a small red pattern and hung by brass rings from the curtain rods. Furniture was bought from the Goodwill, Salvation Army and second hand stores. Furniture such as end tables, rocking chairs and ice boxes. Dressers were purchased new and unfinished and then stained. There were new Skelgas apartment sized stoves, porcelain sinks and light oak kitchen tables with thin red stripes at the edge of the tabletop plus four sturdy chairs in each cabin. The pots and pans supplied for each unit were white enamel with red trim. The dishes were white. Snowy white sheets, dish towels and one large black cast iron frying pan were also stocked. The pan was perfect for frying fish! Mother found a local woman to weave wool rugs in dark shades of red and blue. There was a rug beside every bed and in front of the door. There were also floor mats and window boxes. The cabins were clean, cozy and homey. They were heated by Heatrola stoves that burned wood or coal so there was a coal scuttle and a wood box behind each stove. In the broom closet, a new golden colored broom with a red handle stood ready for action.

Uncle Al, Aunt Lizette, Father, Mother and Anna Marie drove to Shell Lake, Wisconsin to purchase four sixteen foot round bottom wooden boats. These were painted white with red trim. The wooden interiors were varnished and shiny. A used flat bottom row boat of a larger size was bought the first summer. Later on, Father added an Old Towne canvas-covered canoe painted red to the fleet. There was also a goodly supply of anchors, oars, oar locks, rope, minnow buckets and a heavy duty all-purpose wheelbarrow available as well as all sorts of tools. Father bought a used one and a half horse Johnson outboard motor for the girls to use. He said the motor didn't have enough power for them to get into trouble! He already owned an old two and a half horse fly-wheel model Johnson.

The first summer relatives and family helped to clean the swimming area. The shoreline was raked and re-raked as the waves washed in all sorts of debris left by careless people; jars, cans, bottles, old tires and assorted junk were all dumped into the lake. Prior to Father and Mother's purchase of the property, the area, including the beach, the artesian spring and the primitive road had all been used as a public fishing area. The wave action of the lake kept unearthing old debris. Sometimes the girls carried rakes out into deep water to stir up the lake bottom. Gradually, the beach became clean but it was a lot of hard work.

It became evident right from the start that Mother and Father would have to hire help. So in the spring of 1940 Emmett Herranen, an Ely man, began working mostly as a fishing guide for the resort. His brother, Elmer, spent that year clearing land, burning brush and keeping an eye on the resort. Anna Marie loved the two bachelor brothers with sandy brown hair and beards. They were friendly and never in too much of a hurry to answer her endless questions. She followed them around, a little brown-haired eight year old asking: "Whatcha doing that for?" and "Why?" Up the trail they would go a young pesky girl riding on the shoulders of a laughing broad-shouldered man. Later their brother Billy, or Bill, an excellent swimmer worked a summer and taught the girls to swim.

Weekends were extremely busy because Father would be at the resort and there would be big projects to tackle. One of Bill's jobs was to see that the tourists' fish were put quickly on ice in the ice house then covered with saw dust and the spot carefully marked. One day Bill heard Mother calling for him in a frantic voice as he was involved elsewhere on the property. The health inspector was roaming around on his annual inspection and the fish house was a slimy mess!

Elmer and Emmett enjoyed playing cards, especially hearts with Father and Mother. The queen of spades became the Mustamija ("black queen"). Father enjoyed passing that card on. There was much hollering, laughing and pounding on the table during these games but it was all in good fun.

Another character at the resort was Jack Spring, a quiet bachelor who taught mother how to make majakkaa with fish. Jean and Anna Marie didn't like fish stew and slipped pieces of fish to the dog under the table. Dudley Maijala from Winton also worked at the resort. He was full of fun, always teasing the girls and another excellent swimmer. These Finns were followed by Cousin David, Jimmy Toms of Ely, and then Gary Mackie from the Embarrass area who brought along his guitar and sang often in a soft tenor voice around the campfires at night. Sonny Evenochek from Winton was the last of the hired help. Each of these men in turn left a memory of times spent at Back of Beyond, of a special place he was part of.

Anna Marie poked one of the baked potatoes with a stick. They were soft, sort of except maybe in the center.

"Hey, they're done. Somebody find the salt and pepper."

21

Her cousins crowded around, grabbing for the sooty potatoes. They sat on logs, stumps or on the ground eating half-done baked potatoes with very sooty hands.

Delicious!

"Fun, huh? Hey look, the sun is almost set. Means we're done here," Jean said wiping her hands on her snow pants. "I'm tired, that's for sure.

It had been a long day.

That first summer after the cabins were built Mother found inside projects to keep busy. The men, Father and the hired help, took care of clearing the land and trail building. The girls ran errands, played, hauled water, raked trails, piled brush and made wood piles; piles of logs and kindling for the Heatrolas. The piles had to be neat or else they were re-piled! There was time for swimming, fishing and tree climbing. Mother found some stationery that looked like birch bark so she answered correspondence to the resort on this paper using green ink. That lasted until she found tourists peeling the bark off the birch trees around the resort trying to make birch bark writing paper. A big NO-NO!

For Christmas, 1940 Mother sent guests small muslin pillows stuffed with cedar boughs. Sometimes she put a sprig of fresh cedar in with her letters as a pleasant fragrant reminder of the North Country.

The Ely Chamber of Commerce put together a descriptive booklet listing area resorts. The listing for Buena Vista reads:

Buena Vista Resort on Bear Island Lake, 11 miles South of Ely on Highway 21. Pine paneled housekeeping cottages, completely equipped. We have Skelgas ranges, electricity, built in cabinets and closets, porcelain sinks, innerspring mattresses, and coil springs. Fine large boats, excellent sandy beach. Good walleye and northern pike fishing. A real place for a real vacation. We invite correspondence. Mrs. J.B. Kobe, Box 147, Ely, Minnesota.

Suppertime. Early June. Mother was standing by the kitchen window staring at the sunset.

"Would you look at that sunset. Prettier than the one last night. Only one problem. We should have made these front windows ten inches lower. Then I could sit at the table and see the sunset through the trees without having to raise my head. Maybe the loons will be out tonight. We'll stay away from the dock. They don't abide people too well. Guess we best set the table. Where in the world is Father?"

The cabin door opened. Father walked in with a big grin on his face.

"You're not going to believe this, no siree! I was walking down the road at the top of the hill, real quiet like with my hands behind my back like I like to do when I felt something soft and wet licking my fingers. Well, I turned around and there was a fawn, probably born this spring. It was licking my fingers. Honest. I stopped and it jumped into the bushes. Can you beat that? Marie, this place looks like a park, we've worked so hard."

That's as close to a "thank you" as Father could manage. Anna Marie could tell he was pleased and happy. It had been hard work, especially for her parents. The last few months had been hectic. The girls were in enrolled in the Ely schools and the whole family (except Father, who was on the road as a salesman) had stayed in Ely with Auntie Kay and Uncle Joe.

The sun ducked behind some deep purple and pink clouds and night crept up softly. Fish jumped leaving widening circles in the calm dark blue almost black lake. Mother sat quietly in her favorite rocking chair talking to everyone and no one.

"This is so perfect, quiet, birch trees all around, a sandy beach, and best of all-facing west!"

FOUR:
BLIZZARD BIRTHDAY

"Quick, shut the door! Jean, wrap Colonel in that old sweater of mine and put him on your bed. The floors are too cold. Poor dog, no real fur to speak of," Mother said as she unloaded brown grocery bags. "Anna Marie go see if you can help your father haul in those extra hunting clothes he brought along. I'm glad we got here before dark; it's getting colder. This rain may turn to sleet or snow."

Jean wrapped Colonel, her toy Boston bulldog in a torn green wool sweater and gently placed him at the foot of one of the beds. Colonel looked up at her with his bulging eyes, sighed and then snuggled into the warmth of the sweater.

The family had come north to the resort for the weekend of Anna Marie's birthday in November 1940. Father wanted to bring extra clothing for the upcoming deer season, check the cabins and deposit paper sacks of coal briquettes for the wood and coal burning Heatrolas. For the first time, uncles (Father's brothers and brother-in-law) and nephews would be deer hunting at the resort.

"Did you girls remember to bring Colonel's leash?" Mother asked. "We can't let him run loose in this cold rain. Besides, it's getting dark."

"Yup. I stuck it in the bottom of our suitcase," Jean answered.

Anna Marie and Father struggled through the outside door, arms loaded, laughing and nearly out of breath.

"The wind is picking up," Father observed. "Really strange out there. It's been too warm for November. Temperature is dropping and it's starting to sleet. Good thing I brought this coal. I turned the car around so it isn't facing into the wind. Think I better go down to the light plant shed for a shovel and that big can of kerosene. You girls think you could bundle up, get some kindling and fire wood from under the cabin?"

Anna Marie stared at her father. She could tell from the seriousness of his voice that he was worried about something. But what? They were safe inside the cabin. Mother had made a fire in the Heatrola and the cabin was beginning to feel warm. The Skelgas cooking stove was also working perfectly and Mother's homemade vegetable beef soup, prepared at home was simmering over a low flame.

"Well, if it snows the deer hunters will be happy. It's so much easier tracking deer. Just think, Anna Marie you're almost eight years old, getting so big. Soon you'll be as tall as your sister," Father said, leaving the room to attend to business outside.

"She is not! She'll always be a shrimp," Jean insisted.

"Now girls, be nice. No arguing. Will one of you please set the table?" Mother asked. "Did I remember to bring the crackers for the soup? Go easy pouring the milk. We may run out. Before we eat, Jean take Colonel out for a short walk. Don't go too far or you'll get soaking wet. I wish the rain would stop."

Jean and Father came in from the out of doors together. Colonel was nestled in Jean's arms and shivering.

"You're right, Marie the temperature *is* dropping. We'll have snow for sure," Father remarked, frowning at Mother as he spoke.

"Come on everyone. Let's eat! Watch that kerosene lamp. Isn't this cozy with the lamplight and a good hot supper?" Mother said.

"Are we going to home in time for my birthday?" Anna Marie asked.

"I doubt it," Father said. "Depends on the weather. Besides, wouldn't it be fun to be here at the lake for your birthday?"

"No! No birthday cake, no party, no friends, no presents, nothing."

Tears started to sting Anna Marie's eyes.

"We'll see," Mother said through a smile.

After supper, Mother and Father played cribbage. Jean and Anna Marie sat with them at the kitchen table each absorbed in a library book. Logs in the Heatrola hissed and cracked. The yellowish light from the kerosene lamp on the table cast long shadows on the cabin walls and floor. There was a second lamp mounted on the wall in a holder that included a shiny metal back plate to reflect light.

"15-2, 15-4, 15-6, try and beat that," Mother laughed.

She was an excellent cribbage player.

"You win. I quit," Father said, laying his cards down and lighting his pipe. "Best you put those books away until tomorrow. Lamp light isn't too good for reading. It's getting late. Time to turn in."

The girls dressed in flannel pajamas and burrowed beneath warm green wool blankets. Outside the wind raced around the corners of the cabin. Anna Marie fell asleep to the sound of heavy rain falling on the cabin roof.

Then it was morning.

"Anna Marie come open your presents," Mother called out from the kitchen.

"Do I get to open them now? I don't even have to wait until supper?"

Anna Marie tore off the wrapping paper and was pleased to find new crayons, coloring books, a writing tablet and a new fairy tale book from her Aunt Mary in the pile of presents.

"Think you can find enough to do to keep busy?" Mother teased.

"Let me see," Jean insisted as she sat down next to her sister. "Can I color too? Rip a page out of the coloring book. We can share the crayons. Maybe we should play school. I'll be the teacher."

The day passed. Mother had made chocolate cupcakes with white frosting at home and brought them north with the other food. Cupcakes were easier to take to the resort than a full-sized layer cake. For supper they had Anna Marie's favorite: Roast beef with carrots, onions and oven browned potatoes topped with rich brown gravy.

The next day brought blowing and drifting snow. Father decided he should be the one to take Colonel outside. The path he had shoveled to the outhouse kept drifting over making walking difficult. On the night of the "Big Snow" as Father called the storm, he dug out his old harmonica from the pocket of his hunting pants. Time passed quickly. Old tunes from the Great War filled the cabin. Father's foot thumped in time to the music. Mother sat in a rocker by the Heatrola crocheting. Colonel slept wrapped in the green sweater burrowed snuggly in a heap of hunting clothes. No one mentioned the weather. It was just there, pushing against the cabin with wild furry.

Each time someone opened the main cabin door the strong wind blew cold snow into the cabin through the screen door. The cabin seemed to be getting smaller in size, the walls pushing in from the inside while the howling wind and swirling snow pushed from the outside. All those inside gravitated towards the heat source, the reliable Heatrola. No one complained about being cold. They were warm, safe for now and there were four of them, not to mention the sleeping black and white dog. Father had thoughtfully loaded the trunk of his car with sacks of coal briquettes which were supposed to be used by the deer hunters a few weeks later. Every so often Father let his chair to peek out a frosty window, and when needed, tramp to the car to retrieve coal to be added to the wood already burning in the stove.

"This stove hasn't cooled off since we got here. Anyone want a snack? I'll peel some apples," Father offered. "We should have brought popcorn," he added as he stared at the blowing snow through a window.

"Just listen to that wind!" Mother said. "You girls warm enough? You know what? I think I may have a pair of small scissors in my purse. Maybe you want to use them," Mother added.

"For what?" Anna Marie asked.

"We can make paper dolls," Jean suggested.

"How will we do that?"

"Out of drawing paper and the paper grocery bags Mother has saved."

The paper doll project kept the girls busy all that evening and well into the next day. The snow continued to fall piling up around the cabin.

"Wouldn't even pay to try to shovel," Father advised as he opened the main door a smidgen. The slight crack to the outside world displayed snow clinging to the screen door. "The wind blows the snow right back in. The wind is strong. Can't figure out where this storm came from. Sure was nice before this. We'll have plenty of snow for deer hunting that's for sure."

Supper that night was bacon and eggs and slightly brown toast. Toast was difficult to make on the pyramid-shaped toaster that sat on the open flame of the stove burner.

All that night the wind howled. Sometimes big gusts of wind slammed against the three-room cabin walls. Snow infiltrated under the window frames from the force of the wind. Soon the lake would freeze, the first ice forming close to shore. Father had been lugging water by bucket from the lake but with the snow that would be difficult. A summer cabin was not much protection against a winter storm.

Anna Marie woke up early the next morning to the sound of....silence. No wind! The cabin was cool, the fire low in the grate. Father rose, made coffee and re-stoked the fire. Mother busied herself filling cereal bowls with Wheaties for everyone. She poured condensed milk into a large pitcher and added a little water.

"Try this on your cereal," Mother said.

"Just a little," Anna Marie replied. She was crabby. It was only 7:30am! "I can't stand the taste."

"Now hush Anna Marie," Mother said.
Jean glared at her younger sister. Anna Marie was slouched over her cereal bowl.

"Quit being a baby."

"I'm not!"

"Are too."

"Marie, the snow has stopped," Father observed. "I think I'll walk out to the highway. Maybe I can catch someone driving to town."

"Driving? What do you mean? The roads are probably blocked."

"I'll give it a try. Where are my thick gray wool socks? You'll be OK while I'm gone? Girls behave. No fighting. Stay in the cabin. It's really cold out there."

"Jack, eat something before you go. And pull your ear flaps down! Wish we'd remembered to bring the snowshoes."

Father bundled up; first in long gray wool underwear; then wool trousers and shirt; and finally, his heavy read wool hunting coat. Tucked into a pocket of the jacket was his pipe and tobacco pouch. And yes, he did pull down the ear flaps on his black and red plaid wool hat.

Leaving the cabin, Father trudged past the Plymouth buried in snow, eventually making it onto the gravel access road. The snow was waist deep in places. Mother watched Father disappear

28

in silence so as not to alarm the girls. She closed the curtain over the frost-covered window and turned her attention to two bored and restless girls.

Father walked nearly three miles in deep snow in bitter cold. After the "Big Snow" the temperature fell below zero. Father's plan was to walk the county highway towards Ely hoping to find a motorist on their way to town. Houses were few and far between. There was only one other resort located on the road heading north. Luckily he met a county worker plowing Highway 21. Father hailed him and the driver agreed to drive Father back to the resort. The driver was as good as his word, plowing a path right up to the buried Plymouth. The car was quickly shoveled out, started and left to warm up as Mother and the girls hastily packed. All were anxious to get home!

The drive to Duluth was slow. Once home the car was unloaded and the few remaining groceries were put away. Many shovels of briquettes were added to the furnace fire which had burned down to only a few glowing embers. Gradually the house warmed.

Anna Marie sat in a warm bath, a bar of Ivory soap floating by. She leaned back against the cool porcelain tub.

"Hey Jean," she shouted to her sister who was pounding on the bathroom door urging Anna Marie to hurry up. "Were we snowbound?"

"Sure. What's so special about a snowstorm anyway?"

"Well, it was *my* blizzard birthday," Anna Marie replied content to soak in the warm water a few minutes longer.

Footnote:

The "Big Snow" of November 1940 became known as the "Armistice Day Storm", a blizzard that hit and paralyzed Minnesota. Lives were lost. Cattle, wild birds and other animals froze to death. The storm broke all records until the "Halloween Storm" that struck on October 31, 1991. Anna Marie and her family were not aware of any danger during the 1940 event. If her parents were concerned this was not shared or discussed. There was a "Big Snow", cold weather that followed and a brave Father who just did what had to be done: Walk out for help. Years later when retelling their snow bound experience it was always talked about as the time of Anna Marie's "Blizzard Birthday". That the family was in a snug cabin and had ample food, heat and each other was enough.

FIVE:
THE REVOLT

Jean stood up in the aft of a white row boat pulling hard on the starter rope of the one and a half horse Johnson outboard motor. The rest of the boat was filled with laughing, shrieking kids who urged Jean to hurry. It was 10:00am on a beautiful warm July day. It was a known rule that only four people could be in a boat at the Buena Vista Resort. The kids were in violation of that rule.

"Hurry before she sees us," Anna Marie said excitedly. "Get us out of here!"

All the kids were wearing swimming suits. Their intent was to take a leisurely ride around a nearby island. Up on the hill away from the dock a screen door slammed. There was a flash of bright colored clothing. A stern voice yelled out.

"You kids get out of that boat this instant," Aunt Mary hollered.

Aunt Mary, Father's sister was barely five feet tall. She wore granny glasses and was dressed in a blue and white flowered housedress. Over the dress she wore a crisply starched white apron. Her mouth was set sternly. Her arms flapped in the air. Her short legs moved quickly and anchored her body to the ground with sturdy black low heeled shoes. She hurried downhill towards the dock. She was hopping mad! Reaching the dock, she was out of breath. She put her hands on her hips as she addressed the boat load of kids.

"No swimming for any of you kids this afternoon. Now get out of that boat!"

The crew grumbled before slowly abandoning ship. Silently they trudged up the hill towards the resort's store. The store was a haven for the kids, a place to play Monopoly or Royal Rummy on rainy days. When the resort first opened Mother had stocked the shelves of the store with groceries. Now, only pop and candy remained on the shelves for purchase.

Revenge. What to do?

The kids continued to ponder their situation:

31

"Boy, she sure is mean! She isn't fair. We weren't doing anything. Just you wait!"

The disgruntled group sat around the store perched on the counters, chairs or whatever was handy in the room. Anna Marie, one of the youngest in the group listened thoughtfully. She was thinking.

If only Mother were here.

Mother was at home in Duluth running a daycare center for working mothers. It was during World War II and the women were needed in the shipyards of Duluth and Superior or at other jobs vacated by men who left for the military. Aunt Mary agreed to run the resort in Mother's absence during the week when Father was away. And that she did with a firm, but loving hand.

The morning flew by.

"Let's all meet back here at one," Jean suggested.

She had a date that evening and knew that it would likely end up being cancelled by Aunt Mary unless they could change the woman's mind. Someone suggested that they plan a revolt for 3:00pm. Posters were quickly made out of pieces of cardboard.

Down with Aunt Mary. Heil Hitler!

Some of the kids ran up and down the trails between the cabins hanging posters on light posts and trees. A few ran back to their cabins for tin pans, covers and wooden spoons. All of a sudden the War with Germany seemed more real. The kids had seen newsreels at the movies of ranks of German soldiers goose-stepping. Newspaper and radio accounts of the war filled in the details. Pots became helmets. A large upside down kettle became a drum. Wooden spoons became drumsticks. One of the guests contributed an air raid siren. The guest was an air warden back home in Indiana and carried the siren and helmet on vacation just in case of a sneak attack. The siren would be the loudest noise maker! Alarm clocks were tucked under the marchers' arms and set for 3:00pm.

"OK. Let's go. Get in line, now! Hup, two, three, four. Hup, two, three, four. Hup, two, three, four."

Jean led the group single file as it marched up the trail past Cabin One. The curtains inside the cabin moved and Aunt Mary peeked out. She watched as the kids, goose-stepping and pounding on kettles, pots and pans on their heads, marched past. Duke howled when, simultaneously, the alarms rang and the air raid siren went off. The would-be soldiers marched up the trail to Cabin 4 and back down to the store. The summer breeze caused a sign on the door of the store to flutter. It was a picture of Aunt Mary with a Hitler-style mustache! The kids marched into the store and locked the door, waiting for retaliation. The wait was not long.

Aunt Mary climbed the stairs to the store with determination. Her hands were behind her back, her fists clenched around sand she had picked up.

Whap!

Aunt Mary threw the sand at the screen door. It flew back in her face striking her glasses. She threw her starched apron over her face so the kids couldn't see her laughing. Her bright blue eyes filled with tears.

"You darn kids. Now scat and put those pans away!"

Aunt Mary left the stairs. The screen door opened a crack. The kids inside the store feared the worst.

Was she really, really mad?

That evening two car loads of kids from the resort went to the movies in Ely as guests of Aunt Mary. Afterwards she treated them to ice cream cones and yes, Jean was able to keep her date. The kids drove home under a full moon, a soft summer wind blowing. From the back seat of one of the cars someone started singing "Ninety-Nine Bottles of Beer on the Wall." What a day it had been: Revenge and a revolt! But love had won the battle; the love of Aunt Mary for Jean, Anna Marie and the resort kids. Tomorrow the signs would come down and the beach would again be filled with all sizes and shapes of sun-tanned bodies. The revolt was over, perhaps to be forgotten. It had been part of a fun-filled carefree summer during a horrific war.

Somewhere there are adults who recall, maybe vaguely the summer day when they marched up and down a forest trail with pots and pans on their heads while beating kettles and pan lids with wooden spoons. Thanks Aunt Mary for your love and laughter.

SIX:
PETS AND CRITTERS

"You sit on him, hold his legs, just do something," wailed Anna Marie.

Jean pushed the hair from her eyes, took a deep breath and put her arms around a big we, struggling dog. Duke, his nose full of porcupine quills, gave a sigh and rolled over. He had been through this ordeal before. Always in command, Jean told Anna Marie to run and get Father. He'd know what to do. Anna Marie found Father behind the ice house chopping and splitting kindling he had gathered as driftwood from along the lakeshore.

"Hurry, he's hurt. We need your help!" Anna Marie said excitedly.

Father instructed Anna Marie to find a pair of pliers; in fact, to bring several. She headed for the tool chest kept in the small building housing the light plant.

"Hey, old boy. Got yourself into some trouble?" Father asked after he'd approached the stricken dog.

The family and Duke had been through other ordeals: Being lost at night in Duluth; a few fights with other dogs; skunk attacks; and now this, a face full of quills. Duke rolled his eyes at Father and slowly sat up on his haunches. Anna Marie handed the pliers to her father. One by one Father worked the quills out of the dog's nose, jowls and mouth. There was blood. Anna Marie held her breath. It was awful. Her pal, his big brown eyes full of hurt, was being so brave. Soon it was all over. A big pile of quills lay on the ground. Jean gently washed the dog's face with cool water. Mother found him a special treat. Duke curled up in his favorite napping place, a hole dug in the cool earth under the cabin. All in a dog's life.

Duke was half golden retriever and half Chesapeake. A strong swimmer, at times he could be spotted all the way across the bay from the resort methodically swimming after deer who, on hot summer days, had come down to the lakeshore to drink water and escape insects. Though he could easily swim a quarter of a mile, the muscles in his shoulders rolling as he paddled along, the shouts and antics of swimmers off the dock seemed to make him nervous. He would run up and down the dock barking at the swimmers.

Mother always kept a supply of large cans of tomato juice handy for bathing Duke after a skunk encounter. Jena and Anna would don swimming suits, gather up cans of tomato juice, a bar of soap and an old blanket before heading for the beach. Duke was utterly miserable after being sprayed by a skunk. He'd retreat to his hole under the cabin. The girls tempted him out of his hiding place with a bone or a scrap of food.

Mother usually had big soup bones, carrots, a few potatoes and a little celery which she cooked into a dog stew. This was added to Duke's dry dog food. In the spring when the family was busy cleaning cabins and raking trails Duke would appear at the cabin door proudly carrying an old smelly bone he had buried the summer before. He was so proud of himself standing on the porch of the cabin peering in the screen door as if to say: "See what I found!"

Three dogs shared the journey at the resort. First, Colonel Jean's small toy Boston bulldog. Then, Duke the hunter, stalker of squirrels and wanderer. Last Randy, the pest who followed you everywhere, who shared bed space and feasted on blueberries from the very bush you were trying to pick.

One day in early summer Anna Marie decided to go into business for herself. The frog business. Father fastened a wire and screen contraption used for storing minnows to a tree so it wouldn't drift away. The box had a secure screen cover ideal for keeping frogs. Anna Marie got busy catching frogs and stuffing them into a small minnow bucket. When the bucket was half full of the wiggly amphibians the contents were transferred to the holding pen. Jean helped print signs that read:

Frogs-25 cents small ones, 50 cents big ones. Contact Anna Marie.

The signs were neatly colored and hung all over the resort in hopes that the tourists would become customers. But first, the frogs needed to be washed, or so Anna Marie thought. She asked Mother for a small brush and some soap. Mother didn't ask what for. Anna Marie then proceeded to scrub each frog sitting in the pen. There was soap and lather everywhere. Job completed, she waited for customers. Alas, many frogs turned bowlegs up. Others stayed alive floating in the soapy water. Several were rescued by tourists who bought the frogs and later, when Anna wasn't watching they let the frogs go. The business venture lasted two days. Unfortunately most of the merchandise did not.

When the resort was first built and Jean and Anna Marie were still playing with dolls, they had a four legged living doll. It was Colonel, Jean's small black and white brindle toy Boston bulldog. Colonel endured with some patience being forced into doll clothes but he hated wearing bonnets and long dresses. One day Anna Marie got him dressed and settled into a doll buggy covered with a blanket and ready for a ride. It was hard to push the doll buggy over the bumpy dirt trails. Colonel would often escape and Father, in the process of raking trails, would lean on his rake and laugh as Colonel streaked by a doll bonnet over one eye and two young girls chasing him. The girls finally gave up on the doll clothes. Instead, Jean painted Colonel's toenails with flaming red nail polish. Poor Colonel. He was so ugly, he was cute! A few years later, he was given to Grandpa John and spent his retirement years chasing Grandpa's ducks and chickens.

Years later, a car door opened. A light brown streak leapt out of the car. The streak was Randy, small reddish gold cocker spaniel ready to do battle with every squirrel and chipmunk at the resort. What Randy lacked in stature he made up for in courage.

One night, during a violent summer thunder storm, a small bolt of lightning hit the metal bed where Jean and Anna Marie slept. Randy was sleeping with his body tucked against the bed frame. When the thunder clapped and the lightning blazed Jean let out a cry: "I smell something ishy!" The smell was coming from the dog. Randy's hair had been singed by the lightning bolt. A small patch of hair about the size of a quarter fell off the dog the next morning.

Another time, a hot still summer afternoon Anna Marie and Randy were headed up the trail to the cabin. Everyone else was down at the dock sitting in lawn chairs or swimming. Mother had hung an old bacon slab in a tree by the cabin's back door. Randy stopped dead in his tracks. The hair on his neck stood up. Anna Marie absent-mindedly wandered on nearly walking into a bear cub standing upright trying to swat the bacon slab out of the tree. Randy took one sniff and bolted. Anna Marie ran into the cabin and slammed the door. She was shaking. And of course the size of the bear grew with each retelling of the story!

Randy's days at the resort were spent running from tree to tree barking at squirrels and chipmunks who chattered from the tree tops. Once in a while Randy would allow you to rock him to sleep. He would lay flat on his back all four paws in the air eyes half closed a rumble deep in his throat like that of a purring cat. Randy died after eating rat poison someone in the neighborhood back in Duluth had carelessly left out. Mother was terribly upset, fearing that children would get into the poison. Anna Marie and Jean cried. Mother vowed "no more dogs." And Father agreed.

On a shady sloping hill behind the resort covered with birch trees Anna and Jean created a pet cemetery. Whatever was found dead or whatever died from too much TLC (tender loving care) ended up a resident of the cemetery. There were tiny furry bunnies, black moles, baby squirrels and birds with broken wings. The girls weren't too successful at bandaging critters or playing doctor. Mother provided the bandages and advice. When Father was around he showed them how to splint and bandage. Years before while working at the Miller Mine in Aurora he was required to take a first aid course. As a consequence he had infinite patience with the critters and the "nurses".

On her way to Ely one day Mother found several baby skunks running back and forth across Highway 12. The mother skunk had been killed by a passing car. Somehow Mother was able to capture two babies and bring them back to the resort, the skunks riding on the seat next to her as she drove. This was years before the rabies scare. They were so tiny, like new born kittens and needed to be fed with a doll bottle. The girls named them Salt and Pepper. When Father arrived at the resort for the weekend he quietly headed to town to find a vet.

"How soon can we fix them? What do they eat? Are they safe as pets? Can you come out, say tomorrow? I'm afraid we'll get sprayed," he lamented.

A time was set for the vet to come out the very next day. Surgery took place behind the ice house under glass. Father was the chief surgical assistant. The girls waited anxiously at the dock. Salt and Pepper pulled through their surgeries and recovered nicely. They were soon scampering all over. They played in empty row boats and soon began following people around the resort. They were excellent swimmers and enjoyed swimming with folks if they were left alone. The baby skunks had long silky fur little beady eyes and didn't bite or snap. Father built them a cage. The resort kids helped to find frogs, small fish and clams for the skunks to eat.

One day Mother's friend Aunt Em came for a short visit. The girls didn't like her: She was an overbearing and boisterous woman who scared them. She had taught school with Mother in Michigan. Although she wasn't their aunt, many of Mother's lady friends were called "Aunt" rather than their given names. One evening during her visit, Aunt Em sat on a red metal lawn chair at the end of the dock enjoying the sunset. Jean crept up behind the woman and dropped one of the skunks in Em's lap.

"A skunk. A skunk!" she shrieked in panic.

Everyone (everyone that is but Aunt Em) laughed. She left the next day.

Jean and Anna Marie always had a dog pal at the resort. Father saw to it. Mother was tolerant. When a pet died or was sent to Grandpa's to live out its last days another pet took its place. It was nice to have a pet, especially a dog: A warm sometimes wet sometimes smelly body to hug; a wet tongue licking your face. Complete trust and companionship. In the late fall, when the harvest moon was full and orange and the trees were reduced to mere shadows wolves could be heard howling across the lake. It was an eerie sound. Duke, sleeping by the front door would hear the wolves, raise his head and give the family a look as if to say "it's OK. I'm here. You're all safe." And indeed they were.

SEVEN:
THE THINKING ROCK

"See you later," Anna Marie called out to Mother.

Mother was busy at the kitchen sink washing dishes. Anna Marie walked slowly down a familiar gravel tail that connected each cabin of the resort with the store and dock. Head down, she didn't seem to notice her surroundings or that it was a glorious midsummer day. Duke bounded in front of her, occasionally running back for a pat on the head. Anna Marie was headed to the store, where she hoped other kids had gathered, resort kids looking for company and perhaps some sort of an adventure on a quiet summer afternoon.

Funny, she thought as she entered the store, *no one's here. Maybe they all left for town or went out fishing with their folks.*

She admitted to herself that she was lonesome for her sister Jean who had been gone for only a few days.

It's not fair that I can't go to camp. I hate being ten. Let's see. She's been gone since Sunday. It's now Tuesday. Those kids always leave me out. It's always "Be careful. Don't do this. Watch out." Or "Go find your mother if you're gonna cry." Well, I hope it rains all week at 4-H Camp and the bugs are horrible!

Jean was at 4-H Camp on Lake Eshquagama near Biwabik, Minnesota with the Aase kids. The parents had been friends for years. This was Jean's second year at camp. She had earned money to attend by picking strawberries at the Aase farm.

Anna Marie missed her sister. Jean, usually the oldest kid at the resort always came up with good ideas for what to do when there was free time. Anna Marie had to admit she missed her sister at night too. She was used to sharing a big double bed with her. Now there was no one to share whispers with or watch the yellow then white moon move in and out of the dark green pine branches through their window. As a substitute for her sister Anna Marie propped her panda bear on Jean's pillow but he looked silly and forlorn sitting there.

Anna Marie wandered down to the dock sat down on a lawn chair and called to Duke who was bounding after frogs along the beach. Once in a while he managed to catch a frog and then carry it in his mouth for a short time. He never seemed to hurt the frogs. He gave them a short ride before he dropped them.

Watching Duke gave Anna Marie an idea. She rummaged around in the three-sided open shed that was built against the ice house and found the inner part of an old galvanized steel minnow bucket. She followed Duke into tall grass near the shore and after a few minutes captured three green speckled frogs which she quickly plopped into the minnow bucket and set in shallow water. She dipped her hands into the lake and wiped them on her red shorts. As usual her feet were bare: Perfect for wading whenever she felt the urge.

She stood there quietly looking out over the blue lake. The low hum of insects busy in the weeds and bushes was the only sound. A light breeze blew. It wasn't hot.

Perfect.

Anna Marie pushed the fine-grained light brown beach sand with her big toe and watched water lap into the tiny depression she'd dug. There was still no one around. She heard the chore boy chopping wood and kindling in the distance. She didn't feel much like talking to the chore boy. In fact she didn't feel much like talking to anyone. Anna Marie was lonely. Plain and simple. Lonely, sad, and a bit angry that she'd been left out of the fun at camp. Left out. Again.

Anna Marie left the water's edge and slowly climbed the steps towards the store. Inside the store tucked away under the candy counter she had stashed an almost-new light yellow school tablet. She found a stubby pencil and called to Duke.
Off they went. She carried the notebook in one hand. The pencil was tucked safely in a pocket of her shorts. In the other hand she carried the minnow bucket containing the frogs. She and the dog followed a faint deer trail that ran between the cabins and along the shoreline. Duke raced ahead barking. She stopped to sniff and lightly touch the blooms of pink wild roses. The flowers were delicate sweet smelling and soft to her fingertips.

Funny, she thought. *So many times woodsy stuff is soft and when you pick wild flowers, they quickly wilt.*

Father had encouraged the girls to admire flowers, leaves, toadstools and yes, even frogs where they grew or were found. Yet here she was, on her way to her special large rock, which she called the Thinking Rock, with three captive frogs in a bucket.

Anna had discovered the huge odd-shaped rock when the resort was first opened. Tall brush and trees hid it from view even though it was in the middle of the deer trail. From time to time Anna Marie would visit the Thinking Rock and perch herself on top of the boulder. It was safe and quiet: A place to think, sometimes to pout or to get away from her sister's teasing. A place where her mother's voice couldn't reach her to do this or that. A place where other kids couldn't bug her. The rock was her special secret place. She'd told no one about Thinking Rock. She had found it and claimed it. So there!

Anna Marie climbed up the rough scratchy surface of the rock. She brushed twigs and fuzzy moss off her clothing and sat down, opened the minnow bucket and very carefully removed each frog. They seemed a little dopey so she pushed one of them gently with a finger. It hopped a few inches and then sat blinking its bulging eyes. Some resort kids were afraid to touch frogs. Not Anna Marie. When she wanted to show off to city slicker kids she would carry a fat brown lumpy toad in her small hands. Toads were harder to find and catch because they weren't found out in the open like frogs.

So there she sat, a little brown haired girl wearing a white shirt and red shorts admiring three green stunned frogs. She stretched out her legs and looked at her dirty toes. Duke had vanished but she could hear him barking. He'd likely treed a porcupine or some other animal. The frogs sat very still, their green skin twitching. She wished she had some lake water to pour over their small bodies. She thought that they might be sick or sleepy after being in the minnow bucket.

Anna Marie wasn't a bit lonely sitting by herself on her rock. The air smelled sweet like mid-summer. The smell of wild flowers, pine trees and decaying vegetation all mixed together to create the woodsy odor. She looked down at the tablet. The lined paper reminded her of a story she had written during the past year. Mrs. Peterson, her teacher at Merritt School had asked her to read her story, a Pilgrim story in front of the class. It had been a proud day for Anna Marie.

41

At home in Duluth she made many trips to the public library. In the summer Mother, Jean and Anna Marie made weekly trips to the Ely Public Library. Anna liked to read and write stories.

Someday I'll write a book. I'll be famous and people will want to talk to me. Maybe I'll be on radio reading my stories!

Once upon a time there was a woodland fairy princess who lived deep in a green pine forest, under a huge moss-covered gray stone...

She began writing, her head bent over the tablet deep in thought.

"Anna Marie," Mother's faint voice called out. "Come here. We've got company."

It sounded like Mother was standing on the dock commanding Anna to come NOW.

One by one Anna Marie carefully picked up each frog. She followed the trail down to the lakeshore where she stooped over and placed the frogs in shallow water. Each frog jumped into the weeds and was soon out of sight.

"Hey Duke come on. Let's go!" she called out, grabbing the minnow bucket and tablet. She hid the pencil in a crack in the Thinking Rock hoping it would stay there until her next visit. Duke came charging out of the brush, his tongue hanging out, his tail wagging. Wet mud coated his feet and legs making him appear to be wearing high black boots. He'd obviously been busy, snooping in the woods, digging in the muck. The girl and the dog followed the deer trail back to the resort.

"Look who's here," Mother said swishing her hands around her head at gnats swarming around her face. "Mike, Mary, Lois and the other kids are changing. You've got time for a quick swim before supper. We're having a picnic." Mother scrutinized Anna Marie. "Where've you been all afternoon?"

"Just walking around."

"Why are you carrying that tablet?"

"I'm drawing pictures of flowers and stuff."

Anna Marie ran up to the cabin. There was no time to waste. By now her cousin Lois from Ely and the Evenocheck kids from Winton would be shouting, pushing and splashing water on each other. She found her red wool swimming suit on the clothes line, entered the cabin, tore her clothes off, leaving them heaped in a pile on the floor and pulled the itchy one-piece suit over her feet and legs. Before she left the room she hid the tablet under her pillow to read later on, at night when she was alone.

A day that had started out boring and lonely had suddenly become a day to be recalled many times in later years. It had been a day when three sleepy green frogs, a barking fawn-colored hunting dog and a ten year old lonely little girl had shared a summer afternoon. After all, "Once Upon a Time Stories" always end with the phrase "And they lived happily ever after!"

EIGHT:
KERPLUNK!

"Oh my gosh. Here he comes. I could just die! It's so embarrassing. All these people watching. Come on Pat, let's take a boat out. Anything to get away from here," Anna Marie said pushing her friend Pat through the water toward the white rowboats lined up along the shore.

"He's really funning looking in that old suit. Where'd he get it anyway? Pat asked following Anna Marie slowly out of the water.

The two girls launched a boat and rowed out into the lake. The sun-warmed seats of the boat were uncomfortable on their bare legs. Anna Marie leaned over the gunwale of the boat and splashed water onto the boat seats.

"That should help cool the seat off," she said.

"Stop rowing Anna. Let's see what he does."

"I don't care what he does. Why can't he wear a normal swimming suit like other dads?"

"He's just having fun."

"Fun? Easy for you to say. He's not your dad."

Father was walking, parading actually, slowly down the hill towards the dock. Mother and several tourists relaxed in red metal and green stripped canvas chairs in the shade next to the ice house. The dock was strewn with beach towels, bathing caps, bottles of sun tan lotion and bars of soap. It was a late afternoon in August. The air was hot, heavy and still. There was no breeze and no waves. To the west, blackish gray clouds piled one on top of another, billowing, reaching up to obscure the sun.

"Whew it's hot. Too hot to cook. Fish probably won't bite until just before we get rain. Looks like we could get rain later tonight," Mother had said glancing up at the noise of a screen door banging just before Father made his promenade down the slope.

"Here comes our bathing beauty wearing the latest 1940's beach wear. The owner of this resort, father of two daughters and my crazy husband, Mr. Jack Kobe!"

Mother had stood up and bowed as Father sashayed past her wearing a blue and white wool one piece ugly swimming suit. He

44

wore his favorite old straw hat on top of his head. He had an empty pipe stuck in his mouth. Father had returned Mother's bow and slowly advanced into the lake. Once the water was up to his shoulders he turned over on his back and swam between the resort kids. They shrieked with laughter when he stood up, displaying the out-dated suit, the wool droopy and saggy from the water now hung down to his knees.

"What's the matter? You don't like my suit?" he asked. "Well, I do. I've had it for ten years. Ten years. That's older than some of you."

And with that, Father continued to swim round and round the kids who stood in the water watching him.

"Hold my pipe, will you?" Father asked handing his pipe to Jean.

Jean complied. Father proceeded to swim on his back, tilting his head back and drawing in mouthfuls of lake water before squirting it into the air.

"See. A whale. A big blue whale."

"That's enough. Show's over. Come back next year. Maybe I'll still have this suit. Maybe not.

With that Father sauntered up the short path to the store leaving puddles of water behind in the dirt.

The next day after a refreshing night-time rain, Jean, Anna Marie, and Mike the chore boy raked the beach. Father wanted the beach raked at least once a week. The rowboats were pushed away from shore and anchored while the kids rake. Buckets of lake water were thrown over the dock's wooden planking. Sometimes the dock was less than pristine. There was an incident, a time when the dock surface was covered with the innards of clams. Someone had told one of the kids that there were pearls to be found in freshwater clams causing the kids to go pearl hunting. Jean learned that the Minnesota Health Inspector was at the resort on his annual unannounced visit. She made a beeline down to the dock to let the clam diggers know. What a mess! The kids quickly threw the slimy clams under the dock. When the inspector walked onto the dock Mother greeted him with a smile and a "good day." The inspector simply turned and left. That was a close call!

Anna Marie learned to swim by wearing an orange life jacket. Mother insisted Anna wear it, especially the first summer the resort opened, whenever Anna was near the beach. It was a busy time for Mother. She could easily spot Anna Marie in her red wool swimming suit and bright orange life jacket. Anna Marie hated wearing the confining life jacket but found it held her up in the water, which allowed her to quickly learn how to dog paddle. The next summer she learned how to swim. Not well but at least well enough to paddle around after the other kids.

During that second summer Father found a pine log about six feet and eighteen inches around, carefully peeled it and drilled a hole in one side and out the other so a rope could be strung through it. The log could be tied to the dock and pulled up on the beach after use. A kid would sit on each end of the log and teeter totter up and down. Kids swam under it, tried to stand on it to dive off and best of all, rolled over it belly first. It was simple fun!

Most of the resort dogs loved the water. Most, that is except Colonel the bull dog. He was top-heavy and struggled to swim. His little back feet went straight to the bottom as he stood upright trying to dog paddle. Randy the cocker spaniel "fished" with his face in the water for minnows or for whatever caught his fancy. He was at home sleeping on the dock between sunbathing kids. Duke the golden Labrador Chesapeake mix was a beautiful swimmer. Anna Marie teased him by running the length of the dock as fast as she could. Flap. Flap. Flap. Bare feet would pound against the wooden dock followed by a loud "kerplunk!" as she dove off the dock. Sometimes Duke followed her in a belly dive: Ears flying legs reaching for the water. He swam up to Anna Marie, grabbed her by the bathing cap, and towed her to shore.

"Cut that out," Anna Marie would yell.

But it was "no dice". Duke hung on until he had her safely on shore. Rescues by Duke quit when Anna Marie was older and grew too heavy to be dragged through the water.

Pat, Anna Marie's friend from Duluth was an excellent swimmer. She had taken life-saving classes at the Duluth YWCA. Anna Marie was envious of Pat's graceful crawl and diving skills. But diving from the end of the dock was allowed only in early June before the water level went down. And then the dives were limited to belly flops. The water was simply too shallow for a full out dive.

For protection against the hot summer sun Jean and Anna Marie mixed up a concoction of baby oil and iodine. Drops of iodine were carefully added to a bottle of baby oil. The mixture was shaken and then smeared on bare skin. Some summer afternoons there might be twelve bodies sprawled on beach towels on the dock. A suntan was a badge of honor when you went back to school in the fall. Strewn amongst the sweaty bodies were bottles of oil, bars of soap, tubes of shampoo, clothes, books and magazines. Jean would sit on the dock in her one piece blue swimming suit, dangling her toes in the water as she knitted. Anna Marie's favorite swimming suit was a two-piece dark green satin Rosemarie Reid. She wore it so often; she wore a hole in the seat! It was a sad day when she had to throw that suit away.

"Hey Mom, look at me," Anna Marie called out above the din of two outboard motors.

She was calling to Mother sitting on shore watching the kids take turns riding a homemade surf board. Father had found the surf board on one of his boat excursions looking for driftwood. The surf board was really only a small door bleached by the sun. Father towed it back to the resort, drilled two holes through the wood, added some rope, and presto, he'd made a surfboard. Two ten-horse outboard motors were needed to create enough power to get the surfer up out of the water.

Anna Marie stood on the board sailing across the water waving to people on the dock as she passed by. She had a big grin on her face.

Just wait until I tell my friends about this, she said to herself.

Father saw an opportunity to make something from nothing, something the kids could have fun with at no cost. The surfboard kept the kids happy and content. At times, Father also put the kids' creativity to the test.

"We need a few short boards, the hammer and that big can of nails," Jean instructed Anna Marie. "No, not the saw. Just those short boards. Ask Bill and Bob to help."

A log raft was pulled up on the beach. Father had towed the raft back to the resort after finding it in a bay on the opposite end of the lake from the resort. Once he had the raft on shore he bought four empty oil barrels and helped the kids tie them under the raft with strong rope. The kids were attempting to add a diving board to the raft when Jean gave the orders to find some boards.

"Watch your thumb. OK, a few more nails. Look for rough spots so we don't get slivers in our feet."

"Push, Bill," the big sister commanded once the construction was completed.

"Ugh, this thing is buried in the sand."

"Get Bob to help."

"OK now. One. Two. Three. Heave ho."

The raft slid into the lake.

"Hey, it floats!"

Six kids pushed the raft out from the end of the dock, threw the rock anchor overboard and sat down on the wooden platform. But the water was up to their armpits. Too many kids, not enough raft!

"This is fun."

"How about a dive Pat?"

"Well, some of you will have to get off so this thing is higher."

A few kids slipped into the water. The deck of the raft rose above the surface of the lake.

"OK, here goes."

Kerplunk.

A dive off the new diving board. Not much spring to the board but the water was at least deeper than the end of the dock.

"Jean, remember when that dumb kid pulled the top of your swimming suit down?" Anna Marie asked.

Anna was talking to her sister, recalling resort memories, ones from down on the beach in particular, as they sat on the dock.

"No. You sure that really happened? Was it that red and white striped two-piece?"

"Yup. Maybe you don't want to remember."

"No big deal. It happened. So what?"

"Well, it was pretty funny."

"What did I do?"

"Nothing. Just pulled the top back up."

"Who was around?"

"Everyone."

"You mean adults, kids and tourists? My friends?"

"All of them."

"Maybe they didn't notice."

"Well, this kid, I don't remember his name, he came up behind you, grabbed the top of your suit and pulled it down. You jumped up and waved to Mother on shore with your suit floating around your waist!"

"That's not a bit funny!"

"So you *do* remember."

"No!"

The waves of Bear Island Lake rolled in, gently lapping the sandy beach and the flat black rock where Anna Marie baked sand cakes in the sun. Same beach. Same sand. Same view. There were years spent in the water there, horsing around, hollering "last one in's a sissy" ducking in fast, hair plastered to head, teeth chattering if the day was cool. Hours were spent there, having fun, sharing time and the sun with friends.

There was a day, a day late in August. Two more days before Anna Marie was due back at school in Duluth. She held a fistful of rocks and tried to skip flat ones across the water. She held three tiny stones. She tossed them one by one towards the lake.

"Kerplunk one. Kerplunk two. Kerplunk three."

Then it was quiet. The water rippled in small circles where the stones had entered and sunk. Anna Marie turned and walked slowly uphill away from the beach. The air was cool. Summer was over.

NINE:
ROSIE

"Hurry Mother. Here he comes!" Jean had urged.

Mother was in the kitchen. Jean was standing at the front window as she called out to Mother. It was near twilight. The Duluth neighborhood was quiet that early spring evening in May. A maroon and black car standing high off the pavement on four skinny tires pulled up to the curb. The padded roof of the car looked like a smashed blackened marshmallow. Spare tires were stored in wheel wells on either side of the front doors. The car made a chug, chug, chug sound as it slowly rolled to a stop. Father exited the car with a big grin on his face. Mother and the girls stepped out into the cool air.

"Well, how do you like her?" Father asked.

Anna Marie could never understand why cars were always a "her". But that question had to wait. She followed Mother and Jean out into the street. Everyone walked slowly around the car admiring its classic lines. Jean and Anna Marie crawled into the back seat. They pulled the shades down over the windows, opened and closed the ashtrays and bounced up and down on the mohair seat. The car smelled musty and old. The trunk unlocked much like a suitcase. Father sent the girls into the house for a whisk broom. Mother found a bucket and filled it with warm sudsy water. Father attached the garden hose to the outside spigot and pulled it out to the car. Anna Marie was sent to find clean soft rags. Father then lovingly began washing the 1931 Chevrolet.

"What shall we call her?" Father asked.

Anna Marie wondered why a car needed a name. But the more she stood on the curb watching her father, listening to him brag about the car, the more it seemed like a good idea. So "she" became known as "Rosie". It was a logical name. Once an elegant car it was now faded rose and black.

After the car was clean, the old chrome gleaming and the inside swept out, it was time for a ride. They all piled in. Anna Marie peered over her father's shoulder from the back seat as he worked the floor shift. Jean hung onto a braided strap secured near the rear window. Up and down the streets of the neighborhood they went letting old Rosie work her magic on them.

A few weeks later it was time to head north. Mother had been busy packing and re-checking her lists. Clothes were folded and crammed into suitcases. The dog's favorite rug, ball, squeaky toys and dish were stuffed into a paper bag.

"Don't forget the portable sewing machine," Mother called out to Jean who was rummaging around upstairs.

Dolls, doll clothes, a doll buggy, toy dishes, books and crayons were packed into cartons. For weeks Mother had made lists to ensure that nothing was forgotten. Always included, wrapped carefully in several dish towels, was Mother's favorite glass rolling pin. At the last minute Father tied the ironing board to the roof of his company car. Finally they were off, a gypsy caravan headed north to the woods and the resort. Rosie was squarely built so Mother was able to cram the car with clothes and household items necessary for the summer.

Father drove his company car with the dog sitting beside him. The girls and Mother followed in Rosie. There was a sense of excitement, of adventure, but a little sadness too: Sadness of leaving friends and home for three months.

A stop was made in Aurora to visit Auntie Ann, Uncle Jim and Cousins Jim and Johnny. There was much news to share. Auntie Ann was an excellent cook and always had something special baked. She always made them a quick and delicious lunch.

"You've got time for coffee. Come on in. There's cold lemonade and a fresh German chocolate cake."

With that Auntie Ann would put the coffee pot on the stove burner and start digging in her refrigerator.

"You kids go outside while we make lunch," Auntie Ann would say. "Marie, I have part of a potica. I'll wrap it for you to take along."

After lunch and their visit the foursome continued on through Embarrass and then onto Highway 21 to the resort.

Mother seemed proud to drive such an elegant old car into Ely, twelve miles from the resort along the winding paved county road. The car was used as a truck, a vehicle for passengers and a place to escape when one wanted to be alone and quietly read a book. It was also the car in which Jean learned to drive. And of

51

course, a few years later the day came when Jean asked to drive Rosie into town without Mother.

"Now be careful. Watch for deer. And please try not to grind the gears. Hurry back. Don't forget to..."

Mother watched as Jean spun Rosie's tires on the gravel drive and headed for Ely. Anna Marie stood by Mother's side as the car disappeared. She was jealous. She pouted and wondered when it would be her turn.

Sometime later when Mother was behind the wheel driving Rosie, Jean was sitting in the front seat and Anna Marie and her friend Pat were in the back seat. Jean let out a shriek. A small gray mouse that must have been sleeping somewhere in the car was disturbed by the car's movement and commenced to running around on the floor. Jean pulled her feet off the floor and hollered: "Mouse. Mouse." Mother calmly kept driving as the mouse retreated down a small hole by the gear shift. A fried mouse nest was later found and removed from under the hood.

It was a quiet summer night. The moon was so bright it seemed like daytime. The time was near 11:00 pm. Anna Marie and Mother were returning to the resort. Three miles short of the resort Rosie's big headlights dimmed then finally quit. Anna Maria was driving.

"Now what do we do?" Anna asked.

"Stick your head out your side of the window and I'll do the same," Mother replied.

And so they slowly drove home with only the white moon lighting the way. Luckily no deer or other cars were on the highway.

"Let's go looking for raspberries," Mother announced early the next day.

Mother was always on the lookout for berries to pick. She had decided they should search for berry patches along old logging roads. Father made them all berry pails from large coffee cans by adding wire to the cans for handles. Rosie was ideal for such adventures. Sitting high off the ground on narrow tires, she was able to travel down bumpy deserted gravel logging roads. Once a suitable spot was found, Rosie was parked in the shade while berries were picked. It was comforting to look up from the tangles of a raspberry bush and see the old car parked, just waiting to carry hungry, bug-bitten and tired berry pickers back to the resort.

Sometimes the kids snuck away from berry picking to explore old logging shacks. The shacks smelled musty, like rotting logs. Mother didn't want the girls rooting around inside the buildings. That would have been trespassing and a big NO! On these adventures the berry patch was usually silent save for the constant buzzing of insects and the sound of birds flitting from tree to bush.

Anna Marie could never remember Rosie breaking down or having a flat tire. Of course, Rosie was only driven in the summer. She was like a dependable family pet; always faithful. She spent winters down "south" in Duluth tucked snugly in a rented garage.

Driving lessons began in Duluth and continued on country roads surrounding the resort. Jean was the first to learn how to drive. Then Anna Marie. Father, ever patient sat quietly on the passenger's side of the big front seat while the girls ground the gears and killed the engine. Somehow Rosie survived. The hardest lesson was learning to drive Rosie up and down Duluth's hills, always shifting and working the clutch. Father would lean back, smoking his pipe quietly correcting the drivers when needed. There were even a few tears shed when things didn't go well.

Rosie was sold after years of faithful service. She was replaced by an ugly gray Plymouth. Nothing could really replace or be compared to Rosie: To her big headlights, creaking doors, itchy mohair seats and the funny groans and other noises she made as she rolled along. The last Anna Marie heard Rosie had been retired to a gas station in Ely where a snowplow was added to her heavy chrome front bumper. Anna Marie always hoped that Rosie was safe in a garage stored behind closed doors and covered with canvas. Anna Marie thought a "lady" of Rosie's caliber and experience deserved to be driven in a parade but only if it wasn't raining.

Perhaps in the dark of that garage Rosie sighs as she too remembers the "good old days." The days when laughing kids in wet swim suits sat on her elegant but faded mohair seats. The days when, crammed full of kids, the children singing camp songs Rosie came back to the resort after a movie in town. There may even be a few dog hairs left on the floor, some ice cream stains remaining on her seats. Somehow those defects can't diminish memories of a dependable and very classy old car. Rosie is remembered fondly as "truck", the conveyor of family and as a link between the town of Ely and the resort.

Footnote: Potica is a Slovenian bread made from a sweet dough. The dough is stretched thin on a table top. A filling of walnuts, raisins, honey and spices is spread over the dough, rolled up and baked. The result is delicious bread served at weddings, on holidays or at any other large gathering of folks on Minnesota's Iron Ranges. The three locations of iron deposits populated by immigrants who came at the dawn of the 20th century to work the mines, the Cuyuna, Mesabi and Vermillion Iron Ranges are the places where you will still find potica being made and enjoyed today.

TEN:
DO I HAVE TO?

"Grab that handle. Careful now. Help me lift. There. OK. You hang on while I push. Remember the time when the whole thing tipped over. What a mess!" Jean said as she pushed the gray metal wheelbarrow up a narrow trail.

Anna Marie walked beside the wheelbarrow while hanging onto one handle of a large galvanized steel garbage can. Bumpety bump over the gravel path past an outdoor biffy on towards the garbage dump they went. Anna Marie smiled as they passed the compact narrow building. She remembered a few weeks past, when she, friend Pat and Jean were sitting behind that same outhouse smoking rolled up leaves. It had not been a pleasant experience.

Duke scampered ahead with his nose to the ground. The girls brought him along to sniff out any bears who might be lunching at the garbage pit.

"Maybe we should sing real loud or pound on the lid in case there are bears around," suggested Anna Marie.

"You're nuts. There aren't any bears out during the daytime," Jean replied.

"Oh yeah? Who told you?" Anna Marie wanted to best her big sister in an argument at least once. "Well, I don't care. I'm gonna pound anyway."

Bang. Bang. Bang.

Low hanging branches from pines and small bushes brushed against the two girls as they scurried along. The gravel path wound its way for nearly a block, back beyond cabin four, the last cabin on the resort's shoreline. Very quickly the sisters arrived at the dump.

"See. I told you. Look at the mess. Something has scattered the garbage since last week. Hurry up and dump that can. Let's get out of here!" Jean ordered.

The two girls worked together to tip the can and empty it of trash. Anna Marie glanced around, her eyes wide; afraid that she might see a pair of brown bear eyes looking back at her. The girls put the can back into the wheelbarrow and started back to the cabins. The empty can and the wheelbarrow made a racket as they ran quickly down the path to the safety of the shoreline.

At the resort the sound of the cowbell signaled it was lunchtime. The sisters always tried to have their chores done by noon. Finishing their work by noon meant the afternoon was free for swimming, fishing or lounging on the dock reading and sun tanning. Sometimes they would just sit in comfortable lawn chairs and watch the blue waves of Bear Island Lake lap against the rocky shore.

"Now girls," Father said, "after lunch I want one of you to sweep out the biffys and the other to pick up paper and cigarette butts."

Father had crafted a handy stick with a nail on one end for stabbing paper and trash along the trails and in the parking lots.

"Do we have too?" Anna Marie whined. "Can't it wait until tomorrow? We're hungry and tired. How long will it take?" she asked building up a head of steam in an attempt to get out of doing afternoon chores.

"It's her turn to do the biffies," Jean said pointing to her sister. "I did them last week. Besides. I do a better job of finding paper and butts. Father even said so."

"He did not. He told me I did a good job of raking the trails. So there!"

Mother, who was serving them their lunch, became exasperated.

"Both of you be quiet and eat your lunch. The sooner you get going the sooner you'll be done."

There were always arguments between the sisters about who had done more than the other. After lunch Anna Marie trudged up the hill to one of the biffys. She carried an old broom over her shoulder. She had threaded four rolls of toilet paper on the broom's handle. She had also filled the bottle of a pump action fly sprayer with evil smelling bug spray. Once a week all the outhouses were swept, sprayed for flies and had the cobwebs built by spiders destroyed. Once in a while a quick swabbing with a mop was also accomplished. Anna Marie always whistled or sang as she approached each biffy. It was her way of letting folks inside that she was coming.

56

"Hi, Gary," Anna Marie called out to the chore boy a short distance away.

Gary was also busy with early afternoon chores. Today he was delivering big chunks of ice to each cabin for the cabin ice boxes. A pair of black ice tongs was clamped around the ice. Gary delivered the ice in the same wheelbarrow that the girls had used to bring the garbage can to the dump earlier that morning.

Sure hope he washed out the wheelbarrow, thought Anna Marie.

Anna Marie could hear Gary singing in his high tenor voice. She could also hear the sound of the iron wheel of the wheelbarrow as it bumped over the trail between the cabins.

"Hey Gary. Let's clean the boats later on. It might rain tomorrow. Meet you there," Anna Marie called out.

Later that afternoon, Gary, Jean and Anna Marie, all wearing their swimming suits met on the shoreline and began cleaning the resort's three boats. Cleaning boats wasn't a chore. It was fun because it involved horsing around in the water. Each boat was propped up on one side by wedging a spade shovel between the gunwale and the wet sand. Buckets of lake water were thrown into the propped up boat. Scrub brushes were used to clean between the many wooden ribs of the boats. Pails of lake water were then splashed into the boat. Some of the water was splashed on each other. It was a wet, sometimes smelly fun job.

"We should clean the fish house as long as we're so wet. Then we won't have to do it tomorrow," Jean suggested.

The three kids headed towards the small screened fish house located on the shore a short distance away from the dock. Father had installed a small pump that brought lake water directly into the fish house.

"Grab that water bucket and throw some water over there. Where's the wire brush?" Jean asked roughly.

Anna Marie searched for and found the small wire brush. She used it to push wet fish scales toward a hole cut in the wooden counter running the length of the fish house. There was a small garbage can located beneath the hole to catch the debris. Gary waited outside while the girls cleaned the counter. He grabbed a shovel and the garbage can of guts and scales and headed away from the cabins to bury the fish leavings. The girls threw buckets of water across the counter and the floor. Jean held the door open as Anna Marie swept the water out the door. A final bucket of Hilex and water was poured over the wooden floor before being pushed outside. The wet broom was hung upside down to dry.

With a holler both girls ran towards the dock, over the wooden decking and jumped in the lake. They weren't concerned about the water's temperature. They were concerned about the aroma of fish.

"Ick. I even have fish scales in my hair," Anna Marie said. "Did you bring the shampoo?"

"Nope. Just soak your head," Jean said through a laugh.

"You're not funny. I'm telling Mother. All you ever do is tease me. I'm sick of it!"

"Ah go chase yourself," Jean replied, turning her back on her younger sister talking to the other kids laying on the dock sun tanning.

Gary wandered back to the beach.

"Hey you guys want to help me after supper? Go over to Slanty Shanty to look for moss?"

He was looking for company and a few extra hands. Tomorrow he would line fish boxes with fresh moss, followed by ice chips then cleaned and gutted fish. A wooden cover would then be nailed shut on the box. Mother would take the fish to the Ely train depot for shipment to the home addresses of the resort guests. By trial and error they had learned that moss worked better than sawdust. It was a natural insulator.

Anna Marie contemplated revenge on her older sister. She floated on her back watching puffy clouds move slowly through the bright blue summer sky.

Let's see. We got the garbage emptied, three boats cleaned, and the fish house done today. Tomorrow's Saturday. That means cabin cleaning. Wonder who'd leaving? Hope they're out of here before noon. Chores, chores, chores. Bet my friends back home don't have to do anything all summer, thought Anna Marie.

That evening a row boat and the red Old Towne canoe crossed the water to gather moss on the island. Jean let Anna Marie paddle in the front of the eighteen foot canoe.

"Remember when we varnished this thing?" Jean asked.

"And how Father was so fussy, reminding us not to get any dirt in the varnish and how he insisted that we put it on in a thin layer. Two thin layers in fact," Anna Marie offered.

The girls dipped their paddles in and out of the calm water.

"Look. There's Duke along the shore," Anna noted. "That dumb dog will probably swim out here and try and climb into the canoe with us. Don't call him. He'll get tired and give up."

"Let's hurry. These bugs are driving me crazy," Jean replied.

The next morning at the top of Mother's TO DO list it said: "Clean Two Cabins." Mother and her infernal lists! Lists for everyday chores. Lists for groceries. Lists of ongoing chores for Father every weekend.

After breakfast, the girls headed out to clean the cabins. First, they opened all the windows in the cabins being cleaned. A tea kettle was set on the stove and the stove lighted so that hot water would be available for cleaning. Anna Marie grabbed the colorful woolen throw rugs from each bedroom, took them outside, shook them vigorously and hung them over the porch railing as they cleaned. The beds were stripped and dirty bedding stuffed into a laundry bag. They worked as a team during bed making, replacing the dirty linen with crisply ironed sheets, plumping pillows, smoothing green wool blankets that boasted a pine tree woven into the wool before covering it all with a rust colored cotton bedspread. The girls didn't talk much as they worked. Talking wasted valuable time, time that could be better spent goofing off once the work was done.

Next they wiped all the window sills and opened dresser drawers and wiped them out as well. All the furniture was cleaned with a damp rag. Windows were washed if need be. Once in a while a tourist would leave a messing stove or a dirty oven. When that happened it really slowed the girls down.

Anna Marie swept the wooden floors. Jean handled the heavy rag mop and wringer bucket. When the last task was completed Anna Marie would tip-toe across the clean wet floor and hang up three snowy white fresh dish towels and a clean dish cloth for the next guests. The doors and windows of each cabin remained open. Mother would stop by later to inspect the work and to lock up the cabins. She would even check the silverware drawer to ensure that it was free of crumbs and that the silverware was stacked in neat order.

The next day Anna Marie helped Father sharpen axes, knives, brush hooks and his scythe. She hated this chore. She found it boring to sit on a wooden box and turn the handle of the grindstone while her Father worked the steel blades of the implements back and forth. With each turn of the handle the grindstone turned through a narrow box filled with water, which moistened the stone as Father pressed the blade of a tool against the wet stone.

Wonder where Father got this ugly thing, Anna Marie thought. *At least I can visit with Father. Jean can rake the trails. Ha. This is easier than raking and I get to sit down while I work! Just two more axes and we're done.*

Father was fussy about his tools. They were always kept sharp and hung up or put away in a tool chest after use.

Clang. Clang. Clang.

The cowbell rang signaling suppertime.

"We're done. Let's go eat," Anna Marie said. "Mother gets mad if we're late."

"Just a few more minutes and this ax will be sharp. Turn evenly. OK. Tell your mother I'll be right there."

Father headed for the tool shed carrying the sharpened implements.

I wonder what's for supper, Anna Marie thought as she climbed the hill from the lakeshore and followed a well-trodden trail to cabin number four. She noticed rake marks in the gravel, evidence of Jean's work. She sniffed the air hoping to smell supper. She was always hungry, especially after doing chores most of the morning, swimming in the afternoon and helping Father with the grindstone.

"Hey Duke. Come here," Anna Marie called out. "Watchya doin' under the cabin?"

Duke was busy rooting around under the cabin floor.

"Oh no. You dumb dog! No see what you've done? You've knocked over the wood pile. Get outa here."

A small striped chipmunk scatted out from under the fallen wood pile. Duke leapt in pursuit nearly knocking Anna Marie to the ground. She sighed. She knew that tomorrow at the top of Mother's chore list it would read: "STACK WOOD PILE". But at that moment the smell of roast beef beckoned her to walk up the stairs and into the cabin. She opened the screen door and entered the cabin. The door banged loudly behind her. The sound was a signal that the day was about over and that her chores were done.

Chores. Always chores, Anna Marie thought as she sat down at the table and watched Mother slice a juicy roast. *Oh well. It beats being stuck in Duluth all summer!*

"Anna Marie turn the gas down on those mashed potatoes. Pour the milk. Better ring the cowbell again too," Mother said. "Where is everybody?"

"Do I have to?"

"Yes."

"Why?"

"Because I said so."

ELEVEN:
THE WIND HOWLS AND MOTHER PACES

"What time is it?" Mother asked.

The cabin door slammed behind her. Her face was somber. Outside the cabin the tallest trees swayed and groaned with each passing gust of wind. Smaller trees and bushes rustled adding to the symphony of noise. It was late August. A few trees had already lost their leaves. With each new gust dry leaves tore free of limbs and flew through the air. The sun was sort of shining, darting in and out from behind dark rain clouds.

The day had started as ordinary. Just after lunch, the wind came up and the air turned cold signaling that the end of summer was near. Anna Marie sprawled on a couch reading a book. She intermittently watched Mother who had grabbed a sweater from her bedroom closet. Mother glanced at an old alarm clock sitting on a shelf. It was 5:30pm and supper was not started.

"Peel a pan of potatoes and I'll fry the pork chops later," Mother said on her way out of the cabin, the screen door slamming behind her.

What's going on? Anna Marie thought tossing her book on the couch.

She glanced out the window. She could see Mother hurrying down the gravel path towards the dock. Anna Marie walked into the kitchen, dug in a cupboard for the sack of potatoes and sat down at the kitchen table to peel some potatoes for dinner. It was very quiet in the cabin. Only the sound of the wind high in the branches of the trees and the ticking of the old alarm clock could be heard. A few branches scraped the roof of the cabin and made an eerie noise. After the potatoes were peeled, put in a pot of water and set over a low flame to boil, Anna Marie decided to find Mother. She was curious as to why Mother seemed so nervous. She found Mother pacing up and down the dock. It was clear even to young Anna Marie that Mother was concerned.

The wind had stirred the lake into white caps. The resort was located on a bay and usually protected from storms. An island offshore of the resort broke the full impact of the wind blowing down the lake. Anna Marie watched huge waves crash into the end of the dock. They were gray, angry looking, and seemed bitterly cold.

"What's up? What's wrong?" she asked Mother.

"I'm worried. Cabins two and four are still out on the lake. They don't know a thing about handling a boat in rough water," Mother replied as she paced.

The sun had retreated behind dark clouds. Anna Marie shivered as she listened to Mother. Wind always made Mother nervous. Even at home in Duluth far away from Bear Island Lake when the wind came up, Mother would pace.

Duke stood beside Mother at the end of the dock, his head cocked, watching and listening. Behind the crashing of the waves one could hear a faint hum.

"Listen," Mother said.

The hum became louder. Two white bottomed rowboats bounced their way between the island and the resort.

"At least they're together and it's before dark," Mother observed through a smile. "That's a blessing. Everyone is safe."

The boats chugged into the beach and were pulled up as far as possible before anchors were thrown onto the soft wet sand. Suddenly everyone began talking.

"How was it on the big lake? Were the waves high? Did you catch any fish? I was worried you wouldn't get in before dark and then this awful wind came up," Mother jabbered.

Suddenly Mother's face turned white.

"No. No!" she gasped in realization. "Jack is out in that old flat-bottomed boat!"

Father had left earlier that afternoon to gather driftwood from along the shoreline. The wood would be dry and easily chopped into kindling for use in the cabins' Heatrolas. He usually took the older flat-bottomed boat because it was larger and could carry more. He used the old three and a half horse power Johnson outboard motor to push the boat. In years past that same old motor had served Mother and Father on many of their jaunts; trips to the Boundary Waters wilderness, weekend fishing get-aways and finally at the resort.

Mother ran up to the cabin to find a jacket. Once covered, she hurried back to the dock to continue her vigil and to pace. Anna Marie wished her sister would return from Ely where she had gone to pick up the mail and run other errands. Anna was scared and wanted someone to talk to. Instead she paced with Mother wondering if Jean would be bringing mail from Anna's friends. Somehow mail seemed more important than wondering why Father was a few minutes late.

"Run up to the cabin and turn those potatoes off or they'll boil dry," Mother instructed. "I forgot to do it."

Anna Marie walked quickly back to the cabin.

What's the big deal? Father will be back any minute.

She entered the cabin and turned off the stove.

I'm hungry.

She dug her hand in the cookie jar and removed a handful of cookies.

When Jean arrived back at the resort she immediately noticed something was amiss.

"Where's Mother?" she asked struggling through the doorway into the cabin with her arms loaded with two paper bags full of groceries.

"She's down at the dock waiting for Father," Anna Marie replied.

"Where is he?"

"Out collecting driftwood with the boat."

The girls faced each other. Neither wanted to show emotion, to show the other that she was worried. Worrying was Mother's job and she did it all the time. The screen door to the cabin opened. Mother walked into the room. The girls stopped talking.

"I have to sit down a moment. Jean, go down to the dock and watch for your father. Anna Marie, you set the table."

"Why? Supper isn't even cooked."

"Just do it," snapped Mother.

With that, Mother sat down in a big oak rocking chair, her face white and drawn. The rocker made soft creaking noises as she rocked back and forth. Mother's breathing was loud. Her eyes were wet from tears that she was trying to hold back.

'Never again will that man take that stupid old boat out to get that stupid, stupid kindling. We've got plenty of old dry rotten trees all over this place. But no, he's got to go out in that boat and pick up driftwood. So what if it's dry? You still have to find it,

64

dump it into the boat, lug it back here and then split it. I've told him a thousand times not to do this. But does he listen? No!"

The rocking chair thumped. Mother was scared and very angry.

"We'll wait a few more minutes. Then I'm going to ask the men from cabin two to go out with me and find your father."

Anna Marie stared at Mother. She had never seen her mother so worried.

I can't cry. I'm not a baby anymore. Doggone it, I hate this place! All we ever do is work. I'm cold and hungry, Anna Marie thought.

She wanted to cry and stomp her feet. Instead, she sat like a lump on the couch and stared at her distraught mother. In the meantime, Jean and Duke paced up and down the dock. The sun was obscured by rain clouds. The air was cool and fall-like. Jean leaned over and put a hand in the water.

Cold. Too cold for swimming.

Most of the tourists were eating supper. The cold wind made it uncomfortable to sit in lawn chairs and watch the white capped waves slam into shore. Bear Island Lake could become rough when the wind kicked up. Sometimes wind and rain storms from the northwest would stall over the lake up to three days.

Duke began to bark

"Hush up. Sit," Jean hollered, disciplining the dog with a harsh tone.

Duke didn't obey. Jean swatted the dog on his butt. Duke dog sat beside her on the dock and looked at her as if to say: "Now what did I do?"

"Help. Help. Help."

Jean heard a man's voice calling faintly in the distance. At first Jean doubted that she heard anything. The gusting wind forced the voice to float away from her. Then she realized what was happening.

Father is calling for help!

Jean ran as fast as she could up to the main cabin.

"Mother, I heard someone calling for help, over by the island."

"Anna Marie run next door and ask them to come," Mother commanded. "Jean go find some heavy rope. Look in the light plant shed. There should be some hanging there. I'll meet you at the dock."

A short while later, Mother and two male guests of the resort pulled away from the dock in one of the motorized boats in search of the voice calling out for help. Anna Marie, Jean and other resort guests stood on the dock quietly talking to each other.

They found Father between the island and the resort. He was sitting in the flat-bottomed boat in water up to his waist, a silly grin on his face, his pipe firmly gripped in his teeth.

"Hello there. Heard me hollering, did you? Throw a rope over and I'll tie it to my boat. I think you can tow me in."

It was apparent from the circumstances that Father had been trying to paddle the old boat with one oar. The outboard motor had flooded when the wind had come up and nearly swamped the old pram, filling the driftwood-laden boat with lake water. Father's wool pants and jacket were soaked and heavy. Each movement took great effort. He was wedged in the stern of the boat, trapped by the tangled mess of driftwood. Pulling the starter cord of the outboard in his water-logged clothes was almost impossible.

"Jack sit still. Don't try to move. You might force more water into the boat. We'll come to you," Mother pleaded. "Sit still, please?"

The men closed the distance and tied the boats together. Slowly, with the outboard in the rescue boat pulling both boats, they worked their way back to the resort. It was a strange flotilla that approached the dock: A small white boat towing an odd-looking larger flat-bottomed boat piled to the sky with driftwood. Hunched in the back of the trailing boat was a water-logged man with an unlit pipe clenched between his shivering lips.

Supper was late that evening. Everyone was quiet and exhausted from worry. The incessant wind kept them on edge. When night fell the wind died only slightly. Mother talked to Father about catching cold from sitting in a half-submerged boat in cold water in wet clothing. She insisted he bundle up in a blanket. His wet clothes came off and were hung outside the cabin on the porch railing. Father had a difficult time eating supper swaddled as he was head to toe in a green wool blanket.

Anna Marie was silently apologetic that she'd been so crabby about doing a few chores and about being stuck at the resort all summer. A valuable lesson had been learned. A lesson about wind, weather and overloading flat-bottomed boats. Father, an experienced woodsman, had been very close to sinking with the old boat. Then what would have happened? He sheepishly admitted he was afraid to lose his pipe if he had to bail out of the boat. Anna Marie wondered if her father could have made it to shore weighed down by heavy wet clothes, perhaps hanging onto floating driftwood as he tried to kick his legs to safety.

After the dishes were done, Anna Marie sat at the kitchen table trying to read. She couldn't concentrate. Mother had gone to the cabin next door to thank the men again for helping to rescue Father. Father's pipe and brown leather tobacco pouch sat on the kitchen table between Anna Marie and Jean. Jean was quietly writing a letter to a friend in Duluth. The cabin was still and peaceful. Outside the wind blew. Eventually the girls left the table and went to their bedroom. As they tried to sleep, they could hear Father snoring in the other room. Anna Marie looked at her older sister and grinned.

"Not such a bad sound, eh? Remind me never to complain about his snoring."

One thing's for certain, Anna thought as she snuggled in bed. *Absolutely, positively and for sure Father will never again try to harvest driftwood using that old white flat-bottomed boat!*

BACK OF BEYOND: A PICTORAL RECORD

Sisters

Clearing the Land for a Resort in the Back of Beyond

The Road to the Back of Beyond

Paddling Partners

Unfinished Cabin

Resort Sign

Anna Marie Cleaning Cabin

Finished Cabin

Resort Guests

Sisters picnicking in the Berry Patch

Jean & Anna Marie

Anna Marie and Guests after Anna Decorated the Boat with Water Lilies

Kids on the Dock
(Note the Flannel Shirts over the Swim suits!)

Father and the Makeshift Surfboard

Anna Marie and Duke

Going to Town in Rosie

Jean, Anna Marie and Resort Kids

David
(The Promise)

Duluth Girls in Borrowed Letter Sweaters

Gang on the Sign

Anna Marie and Pal Clowning Around

*Anna Marie and Bootsy
in front of Slanty Shanty*

A Farewell Campfire

TWELVE:
TWO GIRLS AND A TIN TUB

In the shadows, tipped upside down under the cabin an old dented tin washtub sat. Anna Marie crawled under the cabin in semi-darkness intent upon retrieving the tub. It was wash day at the resort.

"Ugh! There are spider webs all over it and dirt inside it. Come and help me," Anna Marie called out.

Jean ignored her sister's plea. She was busy stuffing dirty clothes in laundry sacks. Mother had left for Ely; the back seat of Rosie packed to the ceiling with other linen sacks full of laundry. The resort laundry; sheets, pillowcases and towels gathered weekly from all the cabins at the resort bound for a commercial laundry. Mother also brought her own personal laundry to town to be washed commercially but it would return that same day to the resort to hang on clotheslines until dry. This was called "wet wash". The resort's laundry would be dried in town and returned later, crisply ironed, clean smelling, neatly folded, and wrapped in brown butcher paper for storage on shelves in the resort building called "the store" until it was needed in the cabins. There was no rural electrification into the resort so doing laundry without power was a chore. In fact, it was a back-breaking ordeal.

The girls had long ago agreed to that they would make wash day fun regardless; regardless of over-cast skies, bad moods, other more attractive pursuits or pure laziness. Quite simply, there comes a time when you run out of clean clothes. And at the resort the girls' wardrobes were limited. It was the era of blue jeans rolled up to the knees; wearing Father's old dress shirts with the sleeves cleanly rolled up to the elbows and worn over a white T-shirt. Anna Marie was usually barefoot. If she wore shoes at all they were dark brown leather moccasins with white bobby socks rolled down around the ankles.

Hair was another issue. Both girls braided their hair, winding it around their heads or pulling it back in pony tails. At home, much time was spent fussing at night, setting hair in pin curls with bobby pins or clips or, in later years, rollers. But when Anna Marie was young her hair was cut short. She hated wearing it that way and wanted long natural curls like her cousin Bootsy. But that wasn't to be.

"Come on. Let's get going," Jean said after the tub was free of the crawl space. "And another thing. I don't want you wearing my clothes. You never ask. You just take them, then, when I want a clean blouse or whatever, I find it on your back. Keep it up and I'll tell Mother. She'll make you stop."

Jean's eyes flashed. This was a conversation that they'd had many times before, both at the resort and at home in Duluth.

"Well Miss Smarty. Last week you borrowed my red sweatshirt for your big, ha, big date with Andy. Do you think he even noticed? Or cared? Course not. You owe me so don't you go tattling to Mother!"

That seemed to calm the storm. Jean pointed to the beach.

"You go get the boat. I'll lug this stuff down to the shore. Meet you there."

Anna Marie climbed into one of the boats at the dock and rowed it a short distance down the shoreline. She tied the boat to a tree and climbed the hill to the main cabin where she helped her sister lug the washtub, bars of Fels-Naptha soap, a box of Oxydol, wicker laundry baskets and laundry bags full of clothes down the hill to the boat. The process took several trips. The girls were wearing their swimming suits. It was almost impossible to keep dry while washing clothes in a tin tub in a row boat out on the lake.

They rowed the boat away from shore toward the middle of the bay before dropping anchor. Duke, who had climbed aboard for the ride, curled up in the bottom of the boat to take a nap while the girls worked.

First buckets of cool lake water (Father said the lake was spring fed so its water remained on the cool side all summer) filled the tin tub. The water sloshed onto the floor of the boat and onto the girls as they worked.

Next came the whites, which were washed first. The girls took turns scrubbing the clothes on a washboard and applying Fels-Naptha bar soap as needed. They preferred to be alone. They were afraid boats loaded with people might motor up, stop to visit and glimpse the girls' undies floating in the gray tin tub. How embarrassing!

Each piece of laundry was scrubbed by hand and then rinsed in the lake. Once washed and rinsed the wet items were tossed into a clothes basket.

Plop. Plop. Plop.

The middle of the bay was a perfect place to sing at the top of your voice as you worked. Anna Marie and Jean sang robustly all the popular songs they knew as they did their laundry. The "oldies", songs Mother would know were reserved for berry picking. Still they longed for a portable radio. Father had bought Mother a very expensive Zenith portable that ran on batteries and house current. Mother refused to let the radio out of the cabin. It was rarely used as there was too much static. And when the batteries were low Mother would have to wait for the light plant to turn on to use it.

"Wonder what's happening, you know, with the war?" Jean asked frowning at the statement.

Some of her friends were old enough to be drafted.

"I can't stand the newsreels. They scare me. It's so sad, don't you think?" Anna Marie asked thoughtfully.

War news at the resort was limited. Mother relied on the local newspaper, the *Ely Miner*. Father brought the daily Duluth newspapers with him when he came up on the weekends. It was as if they were isolated from the war, sheltered from it all in the quiet woods of northern Minnesota.

Blue jeans were the last clothing to be washed. To rinse the jeans the girls tied one leg of the pants to an oar and floated the jeans in the water. To wring the jeans out the girls each grabbed a pant leg and twisted the opposite direction causing lake water to spray everywhere.

Clang. Clang. Clang.

They recognized the sound of Mother ringing the resort cowbell to signal lunch time. The girls could barely see Mother from the boat as she stood on the back porch of the main cabin. Jean rowed the boat full of clean laundry back to shore. Once the bow stuck land Duke leaped out and charged up the hill followed by Anna Marie and Jean hauling the wet laundry in the clothes basket and the now empty tin tub.

After lunch the clothes were hung out on lines stretched haphazardly between pine trees outside the back door of the cabin.

"Hang all the jeans and the big stuff in front, the smaller stuff on the back lines," Jean reminded her sister.

The undies were thus protected from view on the back lines for modesty's sake. Late in the afternoon if the clothes were dry, Jean would drag out the ironing board. Ironing was kept to a minimum. No electricity meant using a smelly iron heated with white gas. That iron was heavy and air had to be pumped into it to make it burn properly much like a camping lantern. Jean was afraid of that iron. Anna Marie was too young to share her sister's concern. Sometimes sad irons were used as well. But these had to be heated on the Skelgas stove inside the cabin and they cooled off quickly making ironing a slow process.

Because blue jeans took such a long time to dry many wash days lines were strung inside the cabin for overnight drying. Mother especially hated having clothes hung up all over. She said it looked "messy" which it did.

When the wash was done it was Anna Marie's job to crawl back under the cabin dragging the tin tub with her. She turned the tub upside down and sat on the dirt alone in the semi-darkness once more. Duke followed her and rested nearby in his special hole he'd dug in the cool dirt. It was so nice at home in Duluth to open a dresser drawer and find clothes all neatly ironed and folded. Mother was a fuss budget with the iron.

Doing laundry at the resort is for the birds, Anna Marie thought.

Her back ached and her knuckles were skinned from the washboard.

Aha. I know what! Anna thought. *I'll wear my blue jeans for a week and the same shirt for three days!*

Sweatshirts could be worn inside out or reversed front to back so she thought her plan had merit. She changed her mind when she discovered there were some interesting and attractive boy tourists who had just checked into the resort.

If laundry day was warm and sunny and the wind was down Anna Marie and Jean would tie the laundry to the anchor rope or over the gunwales of the boat, jeans tied to the oars, other clothing tied around the boat all gently floating on top of the water as the girls drifted and the clothes were rinsed. What an array! This method allowed the girls to stretch out on the boat seats, read a book or simply let the gentle rocking of the boat lull them into shutting their eyes and dozing.

Anna Marie was always barefoot. Father often teased her saying "I'll have to round you up in the fall and put shoes on you." But she went barefoot because it meant less socks to wash each week.

Today, Anna Marie loads her modern washer and dryer in the basement of her home, pushes a few buttons and walks away, letting the machines do the work. The tin tub has long since been abandoned. Not so long ago the two sisters reminisced and Jean asked "Do you remember the day we were doing laundry and a pair of jeans started to sink? You made me dive in to find them."

Years have passed since two young girls and a tin tub bounced around on Bear Island Lake doing laundry. Surely there must have been an easier way. Perhaps. However it seemed logical at the time. All that water. The clear blue sky. The warm sun. An excuse to splash around in soapy water!

Is there a better way to work on a tan?

THIRTEEN:
SLANTY SHANTY

"Let's ask him," Jean said as she, her sister Anna Marie and their cousin Lizette (known as "Bootsy" to the family) whispered to each other huddled together in a circle.

"OK. You do it," Anna Marie urged.

Father was untangling fishing line from his reel and rod. He looked up as the group approached.

"What's up?" he asked.

"Well," Jean said clearing her throat, "we need some tools to build a shack on the island."

It was natural that they'd appointed Jean as their spokeswoman. She was the eldest. Anna Marie and Bootsy stood next to Jean wondering if their request would be granted. They'd already settled on a name for their island getaway- "Slanty Shanty".

The island, shaped like a hotdog bun and covered with tall pine trees, was located only a short paddle across the water from the resort's dock. The girls and Duke had been to the island many times on scouting expeditions. Duke, who liked riding in the bow of the boat, was always the first on shore. Sometimes, apparently thinking his time was better spent at the resort chasing "critters" or taking a nap under the main cabin, Duke refused to get into the boat. And on other occasions, during the short voyage across the water to the island, Duke would spot something interesting floating or swimming in the lake.

Kerplunk.

Off the bow Duke would go; ears flying, waves rocking the boat as he landed a perfect belly flop. The occupants of the boat always got wet. Water would splash anyone sitting near the front of the boat soaking them from head to toe. Those in the stern would get a mere spray of lake water as the crazy dog performed his dive. Then of course there was always the problem of lugging a soaking wet dog back over the gunwale into the boat. Duke didn't make it any easier, circling the boat, daring you to catch him, looking back over his shoulder as he swam as if to say "leave me alone. This is fun!"

"Well, I can let you have a few nails and some tools but I can't spare any lumber. You be careful. You head for home when you hear Mother ringing the cowbell," Father said thoughtfully."

After helping load the boat with the tools and nails Father stood at the bow thinking things over.

"And don't build any fires. You got it? OK. See you later," he added pushing the boat out into the lake.

Father grinned as the boat began to turn towards the island, likely remembering the "shacks" he built as a boy near Aurora or maybe wondering how long three young girls would "hang tough" before they abandoned their building project.

"Hey look what I found," Bootsy said beaming at her cousins.

"Where'd you get that hatchet? Whose is it? You're gonna be in trouble if they miss it," Anna Marie warned.

"Nah. My dad will never miss it. He only uses it once in awhile to split kindling or hack brush."

Bootsy had taken the hatchet with her from home, concealing it under her long sweatshirt.

Little did the girls know that, as their boat set off across the water towards the island, their cabin project would consume a good portion of their time for several years. Whoever was willing and under the age of eighteen was welcome to help with the on-going construction. No adult visitors were allowed except by invitation! Time spent on the island wasn't all work. There was time to goof off, to perch on rocks at the far end of the island and watch blue green waves roll in. There was time to smell the dry pine needled toasting in the summer sun, time to listen to those same pines rock softly in the wind, almost singing.

Once on the island site selection was the first order of business for the three young female contractors. After scouring the entire island the girls decided to build Slanty Shanty around a stand of nearly dead trees. They chose the site because the dead trees provided them with an outline, a floor plan, already in place. It didn't matter that the trees provided a design with five walls instead of four or that the floor sloped, or, to be more precise, slanted, towards the lake.

Anna Marie and Bootsy began lugging fallen logs to the site. Using fallen logs sped up the process: There was no need to chop down trees. They used the ones already fallen! Some of the logs were so heavy; it took all three girls to hoist them into place. Jean, being the strongest pounded long spikes into the logs while the other two girls held the logs in place. Often times the wood would split as the spikes entered because the nails were too big or the wood would crumble because it was just plain rotten. And then, just as progress was being made during the work day, during the pounding of nails and dragging of more timbers for the walls their work was interrupted by the distant clang of a cowbell. That meant FOOD! The girls would clamber into the boat, their hair tangled with cobwebs, their jeans and blouses dirty, their faces streaked with dirt, tired but blissfully happy. It seemed to the girls that Duke was happy too. He'd explored the island: Now it was time to find his place in the bow of the boat as their maritime mascot.

At breakfast the next morning the girls began their sales pitch.

"We need tarpaper to cover the logs. Something for the roof. And Mother we need furniture and dishes and curtains and glass windows. We need everything!"

The girls pleaded their case. And with some innovation their pleas were answered. Old doors from a leaded glass bookcase that once adorned Jean and Anna Marie's home in Duluth became windows. A breadbox door became a skylight. Tin advertising signs from Father's employer Berwind Coal, three by four feet in dimension, became roofing. Father supplemented the signs with rolls of tarpaper left over from building the resort cabins. Once back on site the girls' rolled out the tarpaper and applied it to the walls. This was a hard job because the paper kept ripping as it was pounded flush against the uneven logs. Then the moss chinking between the logs kept falling out because the nails they were using were too big and the carpenters were unskilled!

Fall came. The project ended for the winter. Another summer arrived. Bootsy and her mother, Aunt Lizette arrived in Ely by train from their home in Illinois. Aunt Lizette had packed old wallpaper, curtains and dishes and had them shipped to Ely. There was much excitement as boxes of "goodies" and luggage were retrieved from the baggage car of the train. Then there was the absolute joy of three girls digging through boxes trying to figure out how to use the contents!

On the island the dirt floor of Slanty Shanty received a covering of linoleum. The walls were papered with the very same lovely green ivy wallpaper that adorned Aunt Lizette's dining room in far off Oak Park, Illinois. The curtains Aunt Lizette had brought with were hung. Cupboards were crafted from wooden fruit boxes and dishes were washed and put away. Despite Father's earlier warning Jean dragged lake rocks into a circle creating a fire ring. Anna Marie and Bootsy lined the trail from the boat to the shack with additional rocks.

During the construction period many willing and not-so-willing folks lent a hand. Some kids just sat and watched the original crew work, repair the shack or come up with ideas for log furniture. For some visitors it was just too much bother to join in what with the getting dirty and all. But to Anna Marie the dirt part was fun; the dirty fingernails, the dirty bare feet, the snarled hair, grubby clothes, skinned knees and the occasional throbbing thumbnail from an errant hammer blow were all part and parcel of the fun.

Cousins Jimmy and Johnny from Aurora visited often. It was always a good time when they came to stay a few days. The cousins became almost like brothers to Anna Marie and Jean. The Slanty Shanty Gang itself was like a family. Jean played the mother. Jimmy, the father. And the rest of them? Mean little kids! At times they imagined that they were a pioneer family settling the wilderness.

One of the tallest pines on the island was selected as a lookout. Spikes were pounded into the tree's trunk for ladder rungs. Someone was always designated "scout lookout" but rarely took the job seriously.

Finally the day arrived when the girls and their friends were ready to entertain their first adult guests. The chore man (Emil or Emmett Harranen) was the first adult asked out to the island retreat. His presence was requested for two o'clock coffee. He arrived on schedule but the coffee was too hours late! It took time to coax a wood fire to the point where it was hot enough to boil coffee.

The Slanty crew was always hungry. If they forgot to pack a lunch or snacks when they left the resort they had to rely upon food stored on the shack's shelves in glass jars. Anna Marie even made Cousin Johnny eat lumpy undercooked oatmeal, something he didn't appreciate. He was only four. The youngest. The logical choice to taste test Anna Marie's cooking experiments. But he was a trooper. He kept up with the big kids following the lead of his brother Jimmy and Jean the two eldest and the ones who took charge of the gang.

Father and Mother never seemed to worry when the kids were across the bay on Slanty Shanty. As long as there was hammering going on the parents knew where the kids were. Even when there were tools missing that hadn't been part of the original agreement Father didn't raise objection. He knew they were needed: Necessary for maintenance and creation.

Then there came the evening when Anna Marie, her best friend Pat (who lived in Duluth and usually spent two to three weeks at the resort each summer) and Jean decided to spend the night at the shack. Three girls and a very wet dog crammed into the small space that night. And of course it rained. The floor, slanted as it was towards the lake and bumpy with tree roots under the linoleum was uncomfortable. Anna Marie woke up in the middle of the storm because water was dripping on her face. It was cold. The kerosene lamp was long dark. The room was deeply black as Anna listened to the patter of the rain hitting the tin advertising signs serving as the roof. Duke growled, the sound coming from deep within his throat, the fur of his neck standing up.

"I think he hears a bear," Jean whispered, waking to the growls from the dog.

"What'll we do?" Anna Marie asked.

"Can't we go home?" Pat added.

"Just keep quiet," Jean answered. "He'll go away. Or maybe it's just a deer."

The girls pulled their blankets up to their chins as they sat staring in the darkness. Duke rose from the linoleum and went to the door.

"Come back here. Lay down," Jean hissed. "Everyone be quiet."

The dog returned to his place near the girls.

Drip. Drip. Drip.

The rain continued to infiltrate the shack and made small puddles on the ugly red floor. The girls couldn't sleep. Finally it was daylight. They collected their gear, loaded the boat and rowed back to the resort. On the mainland the three campers struggled up the hill lugging their wet blankets.

"Well good morning girls. Sleep well?" Mother asked. "Looks like this rain will last all day. How about some pancakes?"

"Can we sleep for a while?" Jean asked. "We heard a *bear* last night. It was real loud too. Duke was growling. We were scared."

Jean was busy telling the story while Pat and Anna Marie stood in the background too tired to care. One thing became clear as the girls talked over their ordeal when they found places to nap in the cabin: They all vowed they would never again sleep over night at Slanty Shanty. It was too risky. Too cold. Too scary. Despite these drawbacks Slanty Shanty became a refuge for the young: A place where kids could isolate themselves from the grownups. But once it was completed and the girls couldn't think up any more projects or new improvements the shack somehow lost its appeal. Perhaps it was because the girls and their friends grew up. Picnics and campfires in more civilized places took Slanty Shanty's place.

Years later at a wedding reception Pat spotted Cousin Jimmy in the reception line.

"Oh there's the daddy from Slanty Shanty," she loudly exclaimed.

Jimmy's face turned beet red but he came over and gave Pat a bear hug. Even that reference is from the past. Slanty Shanty is no more. The walls and tin roof have tumbled down upon themselves, the tin to rust, the logs to decay, the whole pile of debris to return to nature. But despite the advance of years Anna Marie can reclaim images of her sister Jean, cousins Bootsy, Jimmy, and Johnny, other relatives, their friends and tourist kids hauling logs, pounding nails and laughing like there's no tomorrow as the little shack was created. She recalls even more. Damp earth.

Pine scented breezes. The lingering odor of campfire smoke on clothes. Kids sitting around the rock fire ring sharing stories. These are the lingering memories of Slanty Shanty. A five-sided, weak-roofed, leaky shack built of love. Memories strong enough so that when resort kids meet, even today over a half a century from that time they often begin their conversations with:

"Say, do you remember the day at Slanty Shanty when..."
or

"Do you suppose we could go over to the island and see if Slanty Shanty is still standing?"

Of course it will always be there if they want it to be; leaning, wrapped around five dead trees, filled with voices from the past whispering in the wind.

FOURTEEN:
GRAB THE WATER BUCKETS

"Daylight in the swamp. Time to get up."

Father stood in the doorway of the girls' bedroom. He was smiling.

Who could smile and be jolly at seven o'clock in the morning? thought Anna Marie as she stared at Father.

"Go away. Let me sleep. I'm tired. It's too early!"

"Come on now," Father said his voice taking on an edge. "It's getting late and we've got lots to do."

"Like what do we have to do?" Jean asked.

"You'll see."

Father left the doorway. The girls slowly rose and dressed. When they came out into the kitchen Father was frying bacon. The smell filled the chilly cabin. During the tourist season no one was allowed to sleep much past eight. There were chores to be done, and if guests had left, cabins to clean.

Housekeeping the main cabin was kept to a minimum. The floor was swept. The rugs were shaken. The dishes were done. Mother did most of the cooking while Anna Marie and Jean handled the other chores.

Mornings and evenings were cool because the cabins were located close to the lake. To remove the chill each cabin had a Sears Heatrola that burned both coal and wood. These versatile furnaces were either black or brown and the size used in each cabin depended upon the size of the cabin.

That morning no fire was necessary. It felt warm and by noon it would be downright hot.

"How do you girls want your eggs?" Father asked, cheerfully calling out to the girls.

The sisters ignored their father. They were too busy deciding what to wear to answer.

Jeans or shorts? Who cares? thought Anna Marie. *I'm too tired to eat and I don't care what I look like!*

There were two empty water buckets sitting on the ground by the back door of the cabin. The girls recognized the meaning of the buckets' presence. The buckets had to be filled before the day was over. Filled not with water but with blueberries!

"Oh no. Not today," Jean grumbled. "It's going to be too hot."

Mother appeared from her bedroom with a red bandana tied around her forehead. She wore a long-sleeved shirt as protection against the sun and bugs. She too was cheerful. She loved berry picking. It was a chance to wander around the woods with a purpose. Mother would pick all day if she had the time and the berries were ripe. She had terrible arthritis in her hands and berry picking kept her fingers nimble.

"Who else is going today?" Jean asked hoping some resort kids were going along to ease the boredom of a long day in the blueberry patch.

"Well Mike and Mary said they'd be here by eight, so hurry up and finish eating," Mother advised. "Remember to bring mosquito dope and the small buckets," she added before sailing out the cabin door with a determined look on her face likely thinking about the jars of blueberry jam and sauce that would soon line the shelves in the basement back home in Duluth.

After breakfast Anna Marie and Jean made meat and cheese sandwiches and filled a big thermos bottle with cold water before packing the sandwiches, cookies, a few candy bars and ripe peaches in a wicker picnic hamper.

"How come you're not going with us?" Anna Marie asked Father, her voice betraying that she was slightly annoyed Father could weasel out of berry picking.

"Because I have things to do here."

With that, Father never one for long conversations, grabbed his pipe and old straw hat and beat it out of the cabin before Mother could rope him into berry picking.

Anna Marie and Jean shuffled reluctantly dragging their feet in protest down to the dock buckets and the picnic basket in hand. Mother was already on the pier busy, happy as a lark, piling life jackets and additional buckets into the boat. Not a single resort kid showed up! That meant a long day for the girls, a day in which their only company would be adults.

Oh well, Anna thought. *Mike's coming and he's a lot of fun.*

A car door banged. Anna looked up to see Mike Evenochek and his wife Mary walking down the trail towards the boat dock, buckets and another picnic basket in tow. Mike was Auntie Kay's brother. Auntie Kay and Uncle Joe, Father's younger brother, lived in Ely. Mike and Mary lived in Winton a small village east of Ely, the end of the road so to speak. Mike was a big tall man always joking and full of fun. He was a joy to have around no matter what was happening.

When the well for the resort was being dug Mike was there to supervise. When problems developed because the workers weren't able to sink three foot well tiles (water kept gushing in from an underground artesian spring), Mike drove to Ely and borrowed a mine pump. He was always a man of action later traveling to Greenland and South America where he worked with dynamite in other mines and oil fields.

"Hi girls. Ready to go?" Mike yelled trying to be heard above Mother and Mary's chattering.

Mary grinned and climbed into the boat. She was a short lady always smiling and sweet natured. Mother was already in her customary spot in the stern where she could run the outboard motor. Running the motor was part of her fun for the day.

Down the lake they went. It was a beautiful summer morning. Blue waves gently lapped the boat's bow as they moved along. Duke remained on the dock watching forlornly. Father was conspicuously absent likely busy on a project now that he had a whole day of peace and quiet to himself.

There are copper colored cliffs located at the far end of Bear Island Lake. These cliffs sit high above the shoreline. Along the tops of the cliffs the terrain is flat and wide open. In those days, the bluffs were clear of trees due to logging and fires. In those clearings there were blueberry plants everywhere. When the boat struck land, Mother made sure the boat was secured fast to a tree. It would be disastrous if the boat somehow floated away. There were no roads to where they were going to pick. There was only one way to return to the resort and that was by boat. As the entourage climbed the rocky cliff Anna Marie stubbed a toe. She sat on the rocky ground and inspected the damage.

"Come on now," Mother called, "No goofing off."

Of course by then Mother was already in the middle of the blueberry patch busily tugging berries off bushes.

"Pick clean so it doesn't take so long once we get home," she added.

This meant to watch what one picked; no green berries, no dead bugs, no leaves, twigs, or over-ripe berries. Jean picked in silence. She was likely thinking about her current boyfriend, a guy who promised to stop by the resort that evening. She was concerned that they wouldn't get back to the resort in time for her to wash and dry her hair.

"See you later," Mike said. "I'll be back around noon. Let's eat on that flat spot under those pines," he concluded as he wandered off.

Mike didn't squat and waddle through a blueberry patch. He cruised using his two big hands to pull berries from bushes, a bucket secured by a rope around his waist. Though he wasn't anywhere to be seen the others heard him off in the distance singing to himself, their berry picking cheerleader.

"Hey come see this," Jean called out.

She was standing over a rotten log that had been ripped in half to expose a swarming nest of ants.

"Bears," Mother observed. "You kids stay close. No wandering around. If you hear something start singing real loud. That'll scare them."

Oh fine, Anna Marie thought.

The morning flew by. The bottoms of the buckets were covered quickly with ripe warm fat blueberries. Anna Marie and Jean ate more than a few blueberries: They stuck out their blue tongues at each other as they picked. And ate. And picked.

"Time to eat yet?" Mike asked when he wandered back. "I'm hungry."

"OK girls. Let's stop for a while," Mother advised.

By then the sun was directly overhead. Everyone was hot. It felt good to lean back against a pine tree in the shade and munch on sandwiches. Below them the blue water of the lake sparkled in the summer sun. Fishing boats bobbed here and there across the expanse of water. The view from the top of the cliffs was spectacular. Insects flitted in the warm air. There was an odor of pitch and pine and earth and an aura of peace, about the place. It was a perfect summer day. A light breeze blew every so often. No one said much during lunch. They were high above the lake perched on the flat table top of rock and content.

This isn't so bad, Anna Marie thought. *Maybe if we all pick real fast we'll get back in time to go swimming.*

Mother always said that once the bucket was full the rest of the picking went faster. The girls decided to put that theory to the test. After lunch they tried cruising like Mike. But their haste caused them to trample the berry bushes. So they went back to squatting and bumping their butts along the ground as they went from bush to bush.

A noise! Anna Marie jerked her head up convinced that it was a bear. It was only Mike coming towards her his berry pail nearly full. Mike was one who loved to tease and tell jokes. His jokes that afternoon kept the girls laughing. Finally, after hours of deliberate picking Mother was ready to leave.

"Let's go home. I'm tired and the buckets are just about full," she said.

Ah, the blessed sound of those words, Anna Marie thought as they all clambered down the hill towards the boat.

The sun had left the boat seats hot to the touch. Riding across the water in the open boat everyone closed their eyes. Everyone except Mother who steered the boat with her eyes wide open and a big smile on her face.

Father appeared as they approached the dock, ready to catch the bow of the boat and steady it for their exit.

"How many did you get?" he asked.

Mother held up two water buckets nearly full to the brim with blueberries. Mike and Mary did the same. Once on land Jean and Anna Marie headed up the hill towards the cabin. They were tired but not too tired for a quick swim before supper. While the girls swam Mother made coffee for her guests. After coffee Mike and Mary drove back to Winton and their four children. Mike had been a blessing. He'd turned a day of boring blueberry picking, usually a chore, into a day of laughter and good company.

"Will you bake blueberry pie tomorrow?" Anna Marie asked Mother later that evening after dinner was done and the kitchen was clean.

"Yes."

Anna Marie knew that meant a deep dish pie filled with blueberries with a touch of lemon added for tartness. She envisioned the pie its crust made from lard, flaky and golden brown, long before it was made. She knew that the next morning Mother, Jean and Anna Marie would spread newspapers across the kitchen table and clean blueberries. Some of the berries would go into pies and muffins. Some would be eaten fresh on cereal. But most of them would be canned. Anna recognized that the deep blue fruit, some of the berries nearly purple, and all of them tender, sweet, delicious and perfect, were nature's gift to her family.

Was it worth it? Anna Marie asked herself as she sought sleep that evening. *You bet!*

FIFTEEN
OH NO! IT'S JANUARY

Bong. Bong. Bong.

The chime clock on the dining room buffet signaled that it was three o'clock. On that cold early January afternoon the house in Duluth was quiet. Mother stretched out on the couch in the sun porch reading the Sunday newspaper. Jean was off to an afternoon movie with girlfriends. Anna Marie was upstairs studying for an American History test. Father sat at the dining room table writing, pipe smoke swirling around his head. He was staring at a calendar on the table in front of him.

"What do you think Marie? January 14 or 21? I think the 21st is better. It'll give the ice a week more to thicken. We need a good cold snap to make good ice."

"Just let me know how many to expect," Mother replied. "I'll need about two days. No, make that three. An extra day for grocery shopping."

Anna Marie wandered downstairs in search of an afternoon snack from the kitchen. She had one hand in the red apple cookie jar when she realized what her parents were talking about.

Oh no. It's January! Seems like it should still be Christmas vacation. I bet they're talking about making ice. I hate the cold. All the fuss. And that whole long weekend at the resort, most of it spent washing dishes. I wonder if I pretend I'm sick if they'll let me stay home. Nah, they'd never believe me.

Anna was busy scheming, trying to figure out a way to avoid the ice making weekend as she considered her cookie. Father rummaged around the top drawer of the buffet for a scratch pad. Finding paper he put his pencil to it and created two lists. One list for the names of his ice making crew. The other for the food they'd need.

"Same food as last year. OK?" Father asked. "Maybe one more apple pie and some extra butter. We nearly ran out. Remember?"

Mother nodded.

"Fine with me," Mother whispered her face covered with newspaper, her body covered with a brown and yellow wool afghan, sleep coming over her as she replied.

"Let's see. There's Fred. Joe. Jim. Steve. Jimmy. Johnny. And David," Father said writing the names on the pad.

"Don't forget Angelo," Anna Marie reminded from the kitchen, her head buried in the refrigerator.

"Oh yeah. I'll have Steve talk to him. We'll need about ten men plus the cousins."

The following week Father, while working his coal route, stopped in Virginia, Aurora and Ely to ensure that his brothers, brother-in-law and his nephews knew about the weekend selected for making ice. Mother kept a sheet of notebook paper handy to write down the groceries she'd need as well as other necessary items such as flashlights, snowshoes and the toboggan.

When it was time to head to the lake the girls searched their dressers for long wool underwear (which were really Father's long underwear that Mother had mistakenly shrunk), heavy wool socks, flannel pajamas and old wool sweaters. After the car was packed they planned to arrive at the resort early on Saturday afternoon, January 20th. In advance of their trip Father had contacted the county highway department. The county agreed to plow within two blocks of the resort. Father was to lead the expedition, breaking trail from the parked cars into the resort on snowshoes. The others would follow with the men pulling the toboggan loaded with food and clothing.

By the time they arrived at Bear Island Lake and began the trek in it was seventeen below zero! Everyone, even the girls wore pack boots and layers of bulky wool clothing. The boots were rubber and laced in the front with rawhide laces. Several heavy pairs of woolen socks helped fill the void between ankle and ugly boot and kept their feet dry and warm.

"Whew," Mother said after the crew clomped into the main cabin. "It's cold in here. Put all the food on the counter."

"I'll get a fire going in a few minutes. It'll be toasty warm in no time," Father promised.

Oh yeah? Anna thought, stomping her feet. *We gotta be nuts. These are summer cabin and it's below zero outside!*

Father started a fire in the Heatrola before helping Mother and the girls unpack and store the groceries. The men and the cousins went to start fires in the stoves in other cabins. Night fell early. The soft yellow glow of kerosene lanterns set before the windows of the main cabin penetrated the evening, casting faint flows over crisp snow. Lantern light from the other cabins sputtered and waved. The wind died down. The temperature dropped.

It's gonna be one cold night, Anna Marie thought.

"Come and help me," Jean called. "Grab the mattress and lift it so I can tuck newspapers on the springs."

"Why?"

"Mother said to put newspapers between the spring and the mattress. It helps keep the cold from reaching us when we're asleep."

Just before bed the girls made quick cold journeys to the outhouse. When they returned the cabin was warm-sort of- at least from the waist up. But the floors remained ice cold. The bedroom doors were left open to allow the warm air to circulate. The girls donned their flannel pajamas over their long underwear keeping their wool socks on their feet. Before coming to bed Anna Marie tied a blue scarf to her head.

Even my hair is cold, she thought.

Jean was already in bed. She watched Anna Marie climb into the double bed and scurry beneath the covers.

"What's that dumb thing on your head?"

"My night hat," Anna replied. "How come I have to sleep next to the wall?"

"Because you were the last one to get into bed, that's why," Jean answered.

Mother's voice cut through the cold, still air.

"You girls get to sleep. No more talking. I'll be in to blow out the lamp."

Randy the family cocker spaniel jumped up on the end of the girls' bed and spun around slowly as if to find a comfortable spot before settling down between the girls.

"Night, Jean. See ya in the morning."

'Yah, goodnight. Stay on your side, OK?"

"Time to get up girls," Mother said standing in the chilly air above their bed. "We've got lots to do."

Anna Marie opened one eye, looked at her mother and then burst into laughter. Mother looked like a north woods version of Annie Oakley with a green wool scarf around her head, one of Father's faded flannel plaid shirts and a pair of his old black wool hunting pants hiked up over her slender hips and held in place by a wide leather belt. Mother didn't respond to the chuckling. She simply turned on her heels and left the room.

"Hey, Jean, look at this," Anna Marie said, scratching her initials in frost that had infiltrated the room and covered the pine paneling on the wall next to the bed.

"I'll grab our clothes and put them on top of the Heatrola," Jean said. "I'm starved. I wonder what's for breakfast?" she continued eyeing her sister who was pressing her warm palm against the frosty glass of a nearby window.

A few days before the crew's arrival Uncle Steve and a friend of his had driven in to the resort and cleared snow from Bear Island Lake where the ice was to be cut. They did this to ensure that the ice would thicken in the places selected for cutting. The day of making ice the men began their ordeal by chopping a hole in the ice using a steel ice chisel. Once a hole was cut clean through to the unfrozen water below, a long saw was used to cut the ice into square blocks each measuring two feet by two feet and weighing in excess of two hundred pounds. They started the cutting at 8:30am, took a break at noon for lunch and then continued straight through until near dark, approximately 4:00pm. Lake water was poured from the ice house down to the lake to create an ice path similar to the way that lumberjacks used ice roads to move heavy loads of logs during the heyday of Minnesota logging. Using ice tongs with a man on each side of the ice block, the blocks were lifted from the water, placed on the ice path and pushed by the men up the hill to the ice house. In the ice house two men with another set of tongs grabbed the blocks and hoisted them in place forming tiers of ice, six blocks to the tier, inside the ice house. Sawdust that had been pushed to the sides of the ice house would be shoveled on top of the new ice blocks as insulation. The sawdust, left over from a long-abandoned logging operation on the resort's property, had been discovered in the process o f building

100

the resort and had been hauled by the wheelbarrow load to the ice house in warmer weather.

All morning the men sawed and grabbed and lifted and pushed and hoisted the heavy cubes of pure clear ice. They laughed and talked as they worked ignoring the cold. One year Father slipped on the lake ice and fell in after which he made fast tracks into the main cabin. Luckily he'd brought an extra set of winter clothes. He wasn't upset or angry that he'd fallen in. He was upset that he had to strip naked causing a delay and that the other men found his tribulations amusing.

"Hey Angelo," Johnny said. "Want to try my skis?"

Angelo, always game to try something new, left the other men, grabbed Johnny's skis and headed up the hill next to the resort's store. He'd never been on skis. The trip downhill was fast. But, with his legs bowed wide, Angelo managed to stay upright down the entire grade.

"Whatja think of that?" Johnny asked through a laugh as he stood at the bottom of the hill admiring Angelo's descent.

"I go see Marie," Angelo answered. "I'm cold."

Angelo headed back up the hill, this time minus the skis. He followed tracks other men had made in the deep snow. Once at the main cabin he poked his head inside the door, a big grin on his face.

"Hi missus. You got some coffee for Angelo? Maybe with a little somethin' in it?"

"Sure Angelo. Come in. Come in," Mother answered.

Angelo tip-toed, careful not to leave wet snow on the flooring, and stood, hat in hand, his backside to the Heatrola.

"Hi Angelo," Anna Marie said. "Cold enough for you?"

"Yah. How about you girls helping us with the ice after dinner?"

"Can't. We gotta do dishes and pack stuff. We want to leave by 4:30."

"Angelo tell Jack we'll be ready to eat in about twenty minutes," Mother advised cutting slices of homemade pie as she spoke. "Jean hand me those small plates. Anna Marie finish setting the table."

After his coffee Angelo left to rejoin the ice making crew. The women made coleslaw and sliced bread. Some of the food had been prepared at home; baked beans, scalloped potatoes and apple pie had all been cooked in Duluth and then was warmed to eat on the stove of the Heatrola. That evening the warm air of the main cabin smelled of baked ham, bake beans and coffee.

"Wouldn't be the same, ice cutting I mean, without Angelo," Mother observed as she stirred scalloped potatoes warming on the stove. "He's so much fun! Always joking around. Remember last year when he fell head first over the chain across the road? He said he fell because it was nearly dark. I think it was too much Irish coffee. He's sure one funny Italian. And hardworking too!"

"I wonder how cold it is." Anna Marie said. "Randy won't stay out very long."

She glanced at the cocker spaniel curled up on Father's old jacket on the floor in front of the Heatrola. A few minutes later, the ice making crew tromped through the door and into the cabin. Heavy jackets, hats and mittens were piled in corners out of the way. Father mixed drinks and the men found places to stretch out before dinner. Mother, Jean and Anna Marie began piling food into serving bowls and on platters. The men watched as Mother sliced up a pink juicy ham and ladled out heaps of scalloped potatoes. Jean pulled a crock full of brown beans from the oven and placed it on a hot pad in the center of the table. Mother was famous for her homemade baked beans. The women didn't sit down to eat. There were no extra chairs. In addition, they wanted to be sure that the hungry men got fed in a short time. Darkness came early and everyone was tired and anxious to get started for home. The dinner conversation was mostly about the recent deer season, fishing and Angelo teasing someone about something.

"Should be done by four Marie," Father said. "Try to sit down awhile after dinner. Let the girls do the dishes. I'll send Jimmy and Johnny back up the hill with water for the dishes and clean up."

With that Father reached his hand across and gave Mother's shoulder a little squeeze.

It was a long weekend. In past winters, wives of the workers and female relatives would come to the resort for the day.

When that happened the cabin would fill with grownups visiting and catching up on news. Mother never seemed to get rattled no matter how many people showed up. There was always enough food and coffee to go around.

Until the late 1950's, there was no electricity save for that created by the power plant. The REA didn't put lines into the resort until later. This meant that the Koehler light plant was used to provide electric light in the summer. It wasn't used to supply power for appliances such as toasters, irons, ovens or refrigerators. Because of this, it was necessary to cut ice each winter for use over the next summer. Each cabin had its own ice box. Having been purchased by Mother at thrift stores and second hand furniture shops, no two of the ice boxes at the resort were alike. One was a huge green monster; another, dark brown. The others were white. To keep food and beverages cold hunks of lake ice were placed in the uppermost compartment of each ice box. As the ice melted over time water ran through a thin rubber hose to the ground through a hole cut in the cabin floor.

Jean and Anna Marie washed and dried piles of dirty dishes. As they worked the windows became steamed up and the cabin felt like a sauna. Mother sat in her rocking chair with Randy in her lap another year of making ice nearly over.

"Girls, mop by the sink and by the door too where the men tracked in snow," Mother advised. "It's like a lake in here. Just hand up the dish towels. They're too wet to lug home. They'll be fine until spring."

A few hours later the crew slowly retraced their path out to where the cars were parked. The temperature outside was once again dropping as night approached. There was little talking. The men were weary from a long hard day of physical work. One by one the cars started and were left running to warm up. Not a single car refused to start. Father walked over to each car and hollered out a final "thank you" to the workers and then stood quietly watching as taillights moved slowly out of sight against the settling twilight.

"Hurry up Anna. Jump in!" Father urged. "We've a long drive back to Duluth and I want to follow behind the others in case we have car trouble."

"OK, I'm coming."

Anna Marie looked out over the lake from the top of the hill. Her eyes were looking west at a sky that was gray blue. A sliver of reddish sun was rapidly fading behind a bank of purple clouds. She turned and walked towards the waiting car. It was an effort to move her tired legs over the snow after a day of wearing heavy boots. The woods were still. There was no movement anywhere. She felt very much alone and a little sad too, what with the silence and cold all around. No one else remained outside. Even Randy had made a beeline for the warmth of the car. She shivered and wiped her runny nose with a corner of Father's red bandana she'd stuffed into one of her jacket pockets. A hot bath and her cozy bed at home beckoned. She turned her head and took one last look at the cabins reduced by the dwindling light to black silhouettes nestled standing above the frozen lake. She whispered in the cold air.

"Bye for now. See you in the spring."

SIXTEEN:
WHERE'S MOTHER?

A hot humid wind blew in the car windows as Father turned onto
the gravel road leading to the resort. It was Friday afternoon,
5:30pm. He slowed the car and let his eyes focus upward towards
the sunlight filtering through the branches of tall white birches
lining the road. This was the prettiest part of the road. It was cool
in the shade of the birch trees. And quiet. The trees and brush
grew close to the edge of the gravel. It had been a long week for
Father covering his usual sales territory as a traveling coal
salesman. He looked forward to the cool breezes off the lake and
getting out of his business suit and into bib overalls and his straw
hat. Father pulled the car into a parking space by cabin one. It was
quiet. No breeze was blowing on that afternoon. Cabin one, the
main cabin, was empty. There was no one around to greet him.

"Hello. Anybody home?" he called out.

"We're down by the dock," someone answered.

Father opened the trunk of his company car, retrieved his
heavy brown leather suitcase and re-entered the cabin to change. A
few minutes later he emerged and walked down to the lake. There
he found the resort guests sitting on lawn chairs in the shade of the
icehouse. The kids, tuckered out from an afternoon of swimming
and horseplay had spread their beach towels in the shade and were
lying flat on their backs watching black thunderheads building up
directly over the resort.

"Where's Mother?" Father asked Anna Marie.

The girl was eleven years old. She sat on the end of the
dock her bare toes slightly touching the surface of the water.

"I dunno. She said she might go blueberry picking."

"Where's Jean?"

"She's up at the store getting a bottle of pop."

When Jean came down the hill from the store Father
repeated the question. Jean related that Mother had taken Rosie to
a remote lake close by to check out the berries. She'd been told by
someone that the blueberries along that lakeshore were thick and
huge. That's all Mother needed to hear. She'd left two hours earlier
going alone to an isolated berry patch. In her mind there was

105

nothing wrong with going off alone in Rosie over an untraveled road into a desolate lake.

"You mean she went alone?" Father asked his face turning white.

"No one wanted to go with because it's so hot," Jean answered.

"Come on. Throw some clothes on over your swimming suits and get some shoes on. We have to go find her. She should be back by now."

Father was clearly worried. He asked some of the male tourists to follow him in their cars. A slight wind had picked up. There was the smell of rain in the muggy air. The sky was darkening, a sure sign of rain and a likely storm after such a humid afternoon. Father said little as he drove with his two girls towards the remote lake seven miles from the resort.

"Why didn't you go with your mother?" he asked Jean. "You know what a terrible sense of direction she has."

Anna Marie didn't like the tone of Father's voice. She began to cry. She was scared and Father sounded so gruff, so scared himself.

"Stop your crying. It's bad enough your mother is missing. Crying won't help," Father admonished. "We'll need you two to sit in the cars and honk the horns. Don't leave the cars, understand?"

The girls nodded. Anna Marie sniffled.

"Marie, Marie. Why are you so foolish and stubborn?" Father muttered.

He knew Mother had absolutely no sense of time or direction. She'd think that she wasn't lost or confused and they'd be scolded by her for worrying about her.

When they arrived at the lake they found Rosie parked on the side of the gravel where Mother had left her. Father asked the other men to form their cars into a long line. Anna Marie, Jean and two younger boys who were in the other cars were left behind to honk horns while the men searched for Mother. Father instructed them to honk the horns one at a time and not all at once. The air was heavy with moisture. Mosquitoes buzzed through the open car windows. Anna Marie swatted the insects but didn't close the windows because of the heat. The men fanned out and disappeared into the woods.

Father was an avid outdoorsman in good physical condition with a keen sense of direction. Every fall he and his brothers hunted deer at the resort. As a young man he'd spent the majority of his spare time in the woods, winter or summer. Mother, however, was a far different story. She'd loved the woods since she was a young girl. She had very fair skin and sunburned easily and really had no fear of being lost in the woods. Mother had been raised in Oak Park, Illinois, a suburb of Chicago but spent summers in northern Wisconsin. Her love of the woods was almost childlike. She wasn't afraid to wander around or be alone which was very unusual for a city slicker! These things were doubtlessly on Father's mind as he trudged along calling out her name.

"Marie, Marie. I'm over here."

Honk. Pause. Honk. Pause.

Father wiped sweat from his brow with a handkerchief while breathing heavily of the wet air.

"Oh no," he said, feeling the first drops of cool rain. "Please God, oh please hold off the rain until we find her."

He saw one of the tourists off in the distance.

"Find anything?" Father asked.

"Nope."

"Let's circle down to the lake and then back up to the cars."

The woods often grow quiet before a good rain. It's as if all the birds and animals take cover. Father was worried. There was no sight or sound of her. Should they go get more help? What to do.

Honk. Pause. Honk. Pause.

"Let's regroup," Father called out.

The men made their way back to the road and the line of cars. Father looked at his watch. It was 7:30pm. There was still enough daylight to search. The woods remained quiet. The car horns had stopped. Leaves rustled faintly. Bugs flew into Father's face as he tromped through the brush, eyes to the ground, looking for clues. Bent grass. A footprint. Anything.

The men emerged from the woods at the same time. It felt good to be out in the open on the road where the breeze blew easier and stronger. Father walked slowly down the road towards the cars. And there leaning on Rosie, her berry picking hat held tight to her chest, stood Mother. Jean and Anna Marie stood next to her chattering uncontrollably.

"Marie, are you all right?" Father asked as he walked up to the girls. "Where the heck have you been? Why did you come alone? Are you OK?"

"I'm fine," she answered through tears in her eyes. "See?" Mother held up a pail of berries. "I picked nearly half a pail full."

"I am so mad at you for scaring us," Father said.

"I wasn't lost. I knew the road was to my back so I kept walking toward the lake. I thought I heard Rosie's horn. Why are you so mad? I wasn't lost. Not at all."

Father's face was still white and drawn. He finally relaxed and embraced Mother in a big bear hug.

"Let's go home before it starts to pour."

Jean drove Rosie with Anna Marie sitting quietly in the passenger's seat. Father and Mother followed in Father's car. As they pulled into the resort the sky opened up and the rain came plummeting down. Anna Marie dashed from the car towards the main cabin. Once inside everyone pitched in making sandwiches for supper.

"Marie you've got to promise me you won't go out alone picking berries."

"OK. If you insist. I'm not some little kid, you know."

"Yes, but you do get mixed up and it's easy to get lost."

"Who was lost? I wasn't lost. Now leave me alone all of you!"

Mother burst into tears and ran into the bedroom, slamming the door behind her.

Anna Marie went to bed that night with an empty feeling in her stomach. She'd been so scared sitting in that hot car, leaning on the horn until Mother walked out of the woods. Jean was the one who spotted Mother first but they both jumped out of the car and rushed towards Mother as if on cue.

As she tried to sleep the storm deepened.

Crash. Boom. Flash.

The thunder and lightning was followed by the steady patter of rain falling on the cabin roof and dripping from the eaves.

"Hey, Jean, wake up," Anna Marie whispered. "Are you asleep? What do you think would have happened if Mother hadn't walked out of the woods by herself? Boy Father was sure mad. What a dumb thing to do! Who cares about some old blueberries anyhow?"

Anna Marie was poking her sister in the back to get her attention. Jean mumbled and rolled over in their double bed. Anna sighed and scrunched down inside the blankets pulling them closer to her face.

I hope I don't have bad dreams about Mother being lost in the woods and bears chasing her and all. Where's Mother? Oh yes, she's right next door, sleeping, where she belongs. Safe and secure. I helped today, Anna Marie thought, *I really did. Now we're all back together. Tomorrow she'll tell me all about her being lost in the woods. Only, she wasn't lost. Father just thought she was. Where's Mother? Why, she's right here!*

SEVENTEEN:
NOT SO NICE

Anna Marie wiggled her toes, flexed her knees, sighed and rolled over. The window next to the bed she shared with her sister was wide open. A soft breeze stirred the curtains. She watched the moon slowly move between clouds in the open black sky.

"Are you asleep?" Jean asked even though she'd been feigning sleep.

"Nope."

"I can't sleep either," Jean whispered sitting up in bed hugging her pillow.

"Wasn't today just awful?" Anna Marie asked. "I never want to go through another day like this."

The girls could hear their parents talking softly in the next bedroom. Anna Marie knew they were talking about the girls, the resort kids and their recent escapade that had caused so much turmoil.

"What do you think's gonna happen?" Anna Marie asked.

Thinking about what *might* happen to them tomorrow made it hard to go to sleep. The girls knew their parents were both hurt and furious. Mad and sad at the same time. All during dinner the atmosphere around the table had been icy cold. Father remained aloof and carried on a long conversation with the chore boy about deer hunting essentially ignoring the girls. To be excluded like that was awful. Father had locked them out by his demeanor. His sparkling blue eyes were sad and evasive.

The event leading up to the girl's anxiety began a few days before. Anna Marie had trouble remembering why the seven kids, including some of the guests from the resort, went for a walk. They apparently had no destination in mind. They simply set off. Jean was seventeen and Anna was thirteen and they were accompanied by their cousin Bootsy, and resort guests Ken- seventeen and Dave- fifteen who were brothers, and Myrna, nine, and Howard, sixteen, brother and sister. All of the kids were well acquainted. They'd met at the resort in past summers, continued their relationship through correspondence during the winter and were good friends. Friends soon to be thieves.

The day had been ideal for late July. Early evening when the incident took place promised more of the same as the kids started down the gravel road leading out to the county highway. The chattered, teased, and once in a while there was a friendly shove. When they got to a fork in the gravel road they were forced to make a decision.

"Let's go this way," one of the boys suggested.

And they did. The kids were all dressed in blue jeans. The boys wore white T-shirts. The girls wore their fathers' old dress shirts, the sleeves rolled up, the shirt tails hanging free of their jeans. Most of them wore leather moccasins without socks. The girls had braided their hair and pinned it off their necks. Anna Marie kicked gravel as she walked.

"Hey, what do you suppose they're doing back in Duluth?" Jean asked. "Must be boring as heck."

Who cares, thought Anna Marie. *I'm here and it's fun. Besides, I get to go swimming every day!*

"All I know is it's darn hot at home and I'd have to work," Ken, who worked a summer job at a steel mill in Indiana, observed.

The kids kept chatting about their schools, their lives back home and what their friends were doing back home. It was an enjoyable and carefree walk; no adults, no hassles. The road they chose led to three seasonal cabins. The cabins were on property adjacent to the resort but isolated. There weren't many private cabins on Bear Island Lake back then and only two resorts. The area was extremely quiet. The lake was calm as the group approached one of the cabins. Waves lapped lightly against the shoreline.

"Hey come over here and look at this," Dave called out as he looked into the cabin through a glass window.

All of the kids gathered together behind Dave and craned their necks to see inside. Howard lifted Myrna up so she could see too. Inside, the cabin was neat as a pin but sparsely furnished. Unoccupied, the place smelled of wood smoke.

To this day Anna Marie cannot remember who decided to crawl under the cabins just for the heck of it. The buildings were built off the ground without foundations with the land sloped

111

towards the back, away from the lake. All seven of them crawled under the cabin and sat on their haunches talking.

I wonder if this is the cabin Mother and I visited, Jean thought. *The owner was so nice letting me borrow those Nancy Drew books.*

The kids looked up and spotted a trap door in the floor of the cabin above their heads. Of course finding a trap door meant you had to push on it. It opened! One by one, with no thought about the morality of what they were doing, the kids hoisted themselves up inside the cabin. Once inside the kids sat on the floor looking at each other. Jean and Anna Marie began to get nervous and a little afraid. They'd been brought up by their parents to respect other people's property. Yet here they were sitting, uninvited, in someone else's cabin. House breakers! Now what were they supposed to do? It was getting towards dark. The sun was setting behind an island directly in front of the cabin. Someone, Anna can't remember who, opened a cupboard. A wine bottle was found inside and it was one-third full. The bottle and the kids slipped below the floor through the trapdoor and disappeared. The group sat once more on the cool bare earth under the cabin.

"Want some?" someone asked.

"No way," another voice objected.

"Ah come on. Have a swallow."

"Don't be a sissy."

The bottle was passed around. Each of the kids took a slug of awful tasting cheap red wine. The wine brought tears to Anna Marie's eyes. She wanted to cough it up, to spit it out, but instead she swallowed it. The kids crawled out from beneath the cabin. The empty bottle was hidden in a bush. Jean kept the cap from the wine bottle to put in her scrapbook.

As night was falling the crew headed back to the resort. They giggled over the success of their adventure feeling adult and quite smug. When they reached Buena Vista the boys jumped into a rowboat and began to sing loudly pushing, shoving and rough housing with each other. They pushed off from shore in the boat tipping the row boat precariously as they floated. Dave tried to get Ken, his older brother to sit down and shut up.

"Quit showing off or we'll be in big trouble," Dave hollered.

The boys rowed back to shore. "Good nights" were exchanged. The kids all headed back to their cabins after another day of trying to figure out how to grow up, but also, a day none of them would forget.

The next morning a strange black car pulled into the resort. Anna Marie went over the meet the car. The driver asked her if her parents were around.

Oh no, she thought a sinking feeling coming over her, *he's mad about something that's for sure.*

Father was on vacation so that week he was doing maintenance around the resort. Anna Marie ran to the resort store to tell Jean and Bootsy to get going. She suggested that they talk to Aunt Lizette, Bootsy's mother to tell her right then and there they'd broken into the cabin and stolen a bottle of wine. Aunt Lizette was always fair, level-headed and understanding. The girls thought they could depend upon her sweet and gentle nature. She'd always listened to them in the past. Even this time she didn't fly off the handle. She didn't let them down.

"Please come with us when we tell Mother," Anna Marie pleaded.

And so Aunt Lizette accompanied the girls as they reluctantly told Mother their sad tale. Mother's reaction was also predictable; she was near hysterics and very angry.

"How could you? This is just awful. How can we ever trust you girls again? Just wait until your father hears about this," she concluded saying the words the girls did not want to hear.

Soon after their confession to Mother the three girls stood in front of Father telling him the whole sordid story, ending with "We're sorry." By then, of course, Father already knew the details thanks to the stranger in the car who'd figured out it was kids from the resort who'd entered his cabin and took the red wine.

"It was only part of a bottle," Jean explained.

"Doesn't matter," Father said sternly before storming on for a few minutes.

Then he got quiet.

"I am so disappointed in all of you," he said walking away with his head down.

That was it. That was all Father said. It was enough. He was a very fair and honest person. He was also a proud man, proud of his wife and his girls. Knowing this about Father, Jean looked at Anna Marie and Bootsy. She led them all down the small hill behind the store where they all sat down and cried.

The other parents were told. Anna Marie doesn't remember the punishment. She only remembers that for several days Father remained extremely quiet. He didn't make eye contact with anyone. It wasn't so much what he said. It was what he didn't say. Mother on the other hand brought it up over and over and over again. She wouldn't let go of their deception.

Father offered to pay the neighbor for the bottle of wine but the offer was refused. All hoped that the good relationship between the property owners would continue. For several days the kids were quiet; they tried to remain invisible, to avoid the adults. Nothing seemed fun. Even though it was a hot July, the atmosphere at the resort seemed frigid.

As the sisters tried to fall asleep that night after their crimes were revealed, their hearts were heavy. Anna Marie's head ached as well. She was miserable. It was the first time either of the girls had been in serious trouble. The worst of it all was the look on Father's face. It stayed with Anna Marie as she tried to find sleep.

There was no question that Father loved his girls. Not being demonstrative he showed love in a restrained way. Yet his love was always felt. The girls knew they could go to Father and talk things over, things that would cause Mother to rant and rave. It was Father's coolness towards them, his obvious lack of trust that hurt Anna Marie. She knew she and Jean would have to rebuild the trust slowly, over time. They'd done something Father didn't approve of. Anna Marie wanted to feel his love again. She desperately wanted and needed Father's approval, to know she was cherished and loved.

But Anna Marie knew that Father's love would always be there for Jean and her, a constant force in their lives over the years, present during the good times and the bad times, through the laughter and the tears. Father's love would be there for them, even after days like the day they stole the wine, the day they were Not So Nice.

EIGHTEEN:
THE PROMISE

It was a Tuesday. Mother and Anna Marie were returning to the resort after watching a movie in Ely. The night was warm and balmy for mid-July. The moon was beginning to ride high in the night sky casting long streaks of silver across the blacktopped road.

Anna Marie was driving Rosie, concentrating on the road and thinking about a letter tucked in the back pocket of her blue jeans. Wondering. Watching. Waiting. She smiled to herself as she remembered the day Dave and her first met several years ago at the resort. A gathering of young people that night, had, for some reason, congregated in front of an outdoor biffy. For several days before that night Dave had been shyly watching Anna Marie. He hadn't said much to her. Or done much either for that matter. Kidding and giggling the group shoved Anna Marie and Dave into the biffy together. Inside she found herself pressed tightly against Dave. He quickly found her drew her in with his arms and kissed her gently. It was her first kiss. A most pleasant surprise!

Old Rosie continued to chug along. Mother seemed to be enjoying the quiet. She leaned against the passenger door listening to the subtle sounds of night coming through the open windows. Finally, Mother spoke, trying to draw Anna Marie into conversation. But it was hard. Sharing feelings was awkward for Anna Marie. Mother was many years older and somewhat distant. Anna longed to tell her mother about the letter, why she was so excited, why its contents were so important. But she remained silent. The letter made crackling noises as Anna Marie shifted in the driver's seat behind the steering wheel. Over and over and over again she re-read the letter in her mind. The last few lines kept catching her attention:

I'll see you on Wednesday. I'll be driving my motor bike and it's a long trip. Over 600 miles. Watch for me.
Love, Dave.

She turned Rosie onto the road leading into the resort. Gravel crunched beneath the narrow tires. Anna Marie drove slowly as this was deer country. In the headlights a figure appeared off to the side of the road walking on the shoulder. Anna Marie slowed the car. The high beams of the headlights created a silhouette of the figure.

Could it be Dave, hands held up to his face to shield his eyes from the intensity of the lights?

The figure was tall and wore a white T-shirt and blue jeans. Mother, who had been dozing, was unaware of Anna Marie's reaction to the figure or the sudden increase in the car's speed. Anna Marie downshifted and gave the car gas.

Hurry. Hurry.

She parked Rosie in front of cabin one under fragrant pines and told Mother that she was going up the hill to use the "facilities" and that she would be back shortly. Anna Marie's feet flew as she raced up the hill and down the road. Around her the night noises were abundant: Small critters scurried under weeds and leaves; frogs croaked along the shoreline of Bear Island Lake. The moon's silvery silence rode the night sky. But Anna Marie was not afraid. She ran and ran until she slowed to a walk, out of breath.

Is he still on the road? Is it really Dave?

Dave with his short-cropped brown hair and intense hazel eyes usually dressed in blue jeans, Lil Abner boots, and a denim shirt rolled up above his elbows. Dave the first young man who, for some reason, moved Anna Marie with feelings she didn't understand.

Surely it's not love. Maybe a whole lot of like?

She couldn't be sure. She was confused.

Maybe he came a day early, she thought as she reached the end of the gravel road where the road intersected with the blacktopped county highway. Standing off in the shadows was the same tall figure she'd seen when driving into the resort. Her heart raced. She flew into the figure's arms and hugged him. She tilted her head and looked into the man's face. He wasn't Dave at all. He was a total stranger!

Anna Marie sheepishly withdrew, stepped back and mumbled.

"I'm sorry. I thought you were Dave.

The young man laughed.

116

"I'm from the cabin down the road out for a walk. Who are you?"

"Anna Marie from the resort."

They walked the gravel road toward the Buena Vista. The moon was nearly absent, having slipped behind clouds. The young man left her in the shadows near cabin one. It was after midnight. It was Wednesday. Would Dave keep his promise?

Yes.

NINETEEN: SOJOUNERS ALL

A long dark blue four-door sedan leisurely wound its way down the access road to the resort. A canopy of tall birches formed an arch over the gravel road. The car bearing Iowa license plates pulled into the parking lot behind cabin one. Four heavy car doors opened very slowly. A tall man dressed in clean bib overalls and a denim shirt was the first passenger to exit the car. He wore a farmer's cap pulled low over his forehead. At over six feet tall his large frame was anchored to the ground by well-worn work boots. Mother and Anna Marie heard the car's arrival and hurried up the trail to greet the newly arrived guests.

"Hello, Ma'am. Sure is hot," the man said. He gave his name and extended his large hand to Mother. "Sure is pretty here. Cool under these trees." Anna Marie eyed the man from a place behind her Mother. The man reminded the girl of her father's boss. She was terrified of the boss, a giant of a man who boasted a big booming voice.

"We've been driving all night, taking turns, just to escape the heat," the man said before introducing his wife and another couple to Mother. "How's the fishing? We're all so tired. Me and my boys have put in long hours cultivating. I left the work to the boys. This is the first real vacation I've had in fifteen years. The missus says I need to slow down, to rest and fish."

Later that day the farmer would share three foot long aerial photographs of his farm with the others at the resort. His four sons farmed adjacent land. Mother laughed at the thought. To her, a farm was an acre or two. This man's land, including that of his boys covered hundreds of acres and had been in the family for generations.

After a few days of fishing Bear Island Lake the white line above the man's eyebrows, on his forehead, was replaced by sunburn. He no longer wore his farmer's cap when he fished. He was now a tourist.

An elderly couple from Missouri was resort guests for several summers. They were avid fishermen and expert bridge players. Mother and Father played bridge with them on the weekends. Jean sometimes sat in with Mother to make up a foursome. Anna Marie was not even invited to watch. She jabbered too much and the games were taken very seriously. There was absolutely no talking and no eating. Maybe a snack when the game was over. Jean was, by then, in college. It was appropriate that "young ladies" learned to play bridge according to Mother.

"Nuts to that," Anna Marie said.

The small cabin, the one with only one room, cozy, and named the "Honeymoon Cabin" was sometimes actually used for that purpose. One time a newly-wed couple decided to spend their three day honeymoon in that cottage. Jean, Anna Marie and Bootsy giggled and whispered when Mother told them why the couple was at the resort. Their reaction was due to embarrassment, though they really didn't know what there was to be embarrassed about, just that something about the newlyweds would be different after the honeymoon. Given this, the girls decided to spy on the couple.

The honeymoon cabin was nestled in a small ravine. The girls sat on a hill overlooking the area. The only window of the cottage visible to them was a high one located above the cabin's sink and stove. Their curiosity lasted about fifteen minutes. The girls didn't see anything of note. Nothing happened. No one was spotted in the altogether. It was simply quiet. So ended the spying episode.

The Fourth of July was usually quiet and spent at the resort. It was war time. There wasn't extra gasoline to drive around looking for a parade. Father's relatives came out for the day to swim, loaf, fish and share a picnic supper. A huge watermelon was kept cold by immersing it in the overflow of an icy spring captured in a hole dug in the ground near the minnow tank. Sometimes after the picnic the kids played with sparklers in the dark. This quiet celebration ended one year when a guest supplied a small carbide cannon, a "thank you" gift to Father and Mother for ensuring the guests a nice vacation. The cannon sat on three thin metal legs and was cranked by hand.

"Anna Marie," Father would order. "Clear off the dock. Give it a quick sweep with the broom from the fish house so nothing will catch fire. You kids stand clear and cover your ears," Father would continue kneeling next to the cannon. He would begin to crank the ridiculously little device like a madman. "OK. Here we go," he'd warn. "Ready?"

Boom. Boom. Boom.

Duke would run and hide. The sound was thunderously gloriously loud! The smell of burnt carbide would hang in the thick evening air.

Sometimes Mother made homemade ice cream to celebrate the Fourth. Anyone, tourists, family or passersby who were willing and able to help turn the crank of the ice cream maker were welcome to join in. The universally favorite flavor was fresh peach. The greatest reward? Licking the device's beaters before anyone else had a taste.

The resort had virtually no advertising budget. Mother depended upon word-of-mouth and limited newspaper ads to fill the cabins for the short summer tourist season. When letters reserving cabins came Anna Marie and Jean were always curious?

"Do they have any kids?"

And when the cars filled with guests eventually arrived, there was always a short awkward time during which everyone was introduced. The quiet beauty of the woods, the shade of the trees and the sparkling water of the lake instantly relaxed nervous guests. The tourists couldn't wait to unpack so that they could get out on the lake to fish or sit in lawn chairs to watch the waves. Tourist kids were shy at first as they got to know the girls and the others already at the resort. By the second day, plans were formed to meet at the dock for swimming or sitting around, talking, learning about one another. Both kids and adults started to unwind, to relax.

Because of the war and gas rationing vacations had to be planned well in advance. Tires were scarce. Somehow, someway folks drove up from Iowa, Illinois, Missouri, Wisconsin, Indiana and southern Minnesota to find peace and quiet at the resort. But even then, against the serenity of Bear Island Lake the war was ever present. The guests and hosts at Buena Vista could not escape news of the war contained in radio reports, newsreels at the movie houses or in the letters home from servicemen. Even still, a vacation in the north woods of Minnesota spent at a family-owned resort allowed an oasis from reality, respite from the ugliness of war.

Mother had a close friend whose husband was a Lieutenant Colonel in the Army. He was fighting the war in Italy. Anna Marie remembers the day the war came home for her. The woman was at the resort, in Mother's arms, sobbing. Her husband had been captured and thrown into a prisoner of war camp in Italy by the Fascists. And there had been no word. No letters. Only silence from him since his capture. Then a letter came. He'd been released from the camp. When he came home, Mother suggested that the couple spend time at the resort. By then it was fall and the resort was officially closed. But because he was weak in body and drained of spirit, that made it perfect. The resort afforded the man and his wife complete peace and quiet. There were no guns. No rolling tanks. No bad memories of war to haunt him. The couple spent a week at the resort. They threw open the windows despite autumn's chill, open to hear the waves beat against the shore, to hear the trees groan in the wind. The two of them, bruised sojourners, had the place to themselves. The absolute healing power of the woods worked magic on the battered serviceman just as it healed ordinary tourists.

Mother kept a guest book. Inside its covers the book contained many names, many memories. Often tourists would return as guests year after year. Friendships were forged, some lasting over fifty years, some severed by time and distance. Boy and girl, man and woman romances flourished there then died. Years later, kids who'd been guests returned for their honeymoon at the resort or for camping trips on the islands of Bear Island Lake. Mother also kept photo albums of those times. Snapshots helped focus hazy memories.

"Say, do you remember the Bates? The Dicks. The Kings?"

"I wonder where they are now. Get a load of the hairdos. The clothes. Can you believe we wore that stuff? "

"I'll never forget the time Anna Marie stuck water lilies in all the gunwales of the boats. Real pretty. "

"And the eight pound walleye that Aunt Lizette caught!"

"And Pat. And Jean. And Bootsy. And Bill. And Bob. And Gary all spread out on the dock in their suits soaking up the sun."

Sojourners all, bumping into each other, sharing lives, building memories at a place that was so special, you needed a reservation!

TWENTY:
TALES AROUND THE TABLE

"Anna Marie run to the top of the hill where Rosie is parked. I saw some ripe blueberries up there, along the road. We only need two cups for muffins," Mother said. "Jean light the oven and set it at 350°. We'll have to hurry. They'll be here by one or so. So much to do! Keep the dog inside. I just swept the floor. I think I'll sit a minute and finish my morning coffee. Jean, you want a cup?"

"No. I'll start measuring for the muffins," Jean replied. "Anna Marie can set the table. It's only fair cuz' I peeled the spuds. Let's see:

Two cups sifted flour
One-quarter teaspoons salt
Two teaspoons baking powder
One-half cup sugar
One-quarter cup butter
Two eggs, separated
One cup milk
One to two cups blueberries.

Now what I do?" Jean asked, reading from Aunt Mary's recipe for her famous blueberry muffins.

"Sift the dry ingredients together. Cream the butter and add the sugar. Add the beaten egg yolks to the sugar and butter. Then add the dry ingredients and the milk. When Anna Marie returns with the berries make sure they get washed and dried on a towel. They need to be rolled in flour and added to the batter. Beat the egg whites frothy and fold them into the batter. Remember to grease the muffin tins. They take about fifteen minutes to bake. We'll get at least two dozen muffins. Think you can handle it?" Mother asked her eldest daughter. "Just let me finish my coffee then I'll start frying fish."

Mother watched Jean work in the kitchen through a smile. The day had finally arrived. It was the second Sunday in August and her brother Al, his wife Lizette and their daughter Boosty (one month younger than Anna Marie) would arrive from Oak Park, Illinois intending to stay for two weeks. But first they would be treated to a dinner carefully planned by Mother followed by lots of time for "table talk."

Her coffee cup empty, the muffins baking in the oven Mother went to work. She shook the walleye fillets carefully in a brown paper bag filled with flour and cornmeal. She heated Crisco in a frying pan on the range, gently adding the fillets to the pan, frying them until golden brown and crunchy. It helped to use a big black skillet. The fish was turned over only once and then gently place on cookie sheets slid into the oven on low heat to keep the fish warm. New potatoes would be boiled and drizzled with butter, parsley, salt and pepper. Mother would also boil corn on the cob, toss a big vegetable salad and keep the muffins warm for the table. For dessert Mother had saved a juicy red and ice cold watermelon. There was some thought to a lemon meringue pie but the oven was in use warming the fish.

The Dick brothers from Iowa, Illinois and Minnesota had checked out of the resort on Saturday. These three families of avid fishermen had kept everyone at the resort supplied with walleye and northern pike fillets. They fished every single day of their vacation until one or two in the afternoon, spending the rest of their day exploring the countryside in and around Ely.

It had been a busy week. The girls had helped Mother can two lugs of peaches and a lug of pears. Pint and quart jars of fruit sauce were readied so that Father could haul them back to Duluth where they would be placed in a cool basement storage cupboard. The next week, the women would pick blueberries and the tangy smell of blueberry jam bubbling on the cabin's stove would fill the cabin. Some berries were made into sauce. The rest into jam. One summer, Mother tried freezing blueberries, storing them in a locker plant in Ely. But Mother found the berries too hard that way. She called them "blue bullets."

"Here they are now," Mother said hearing the approach of a car. The girls and their parents walked out to greet the Barber family. "Come on in. Everything's ready. How was your trip?" Mother asked hugging her brother and sister-in-law. "My how you've grown Bootsy. The girls have been waiting for you!"

The crew entered cabin one.

"Everyone sit down," Mother commanded. "Jack take your usual place. Al and Lizette can sit by me. The kids can sit on the bench. Our new chore boy Jimmy Toms should be here in a minute."

"Marie I've waited a whole year to taste fish this good," Uncle Al said. "Bear Island Lake has to be one of the best walleye lakes around. Remember last year, when Lizette caught that eight-pounder? Never saw such a big walleye. She about fainted right in the boat! Glad she didn't. We probably would have had to haul her back in after she fell overboard. Fainting'll do that, you know!" Al concluded glancing at his pretty dark haired wife.

Aunty Lizette smiled back. She loved the teasing.

"If we eat any more, we'll have to build a bigger table and buy bigger chairs," Father announced. "Everyone had enough fish? More corn anyone?"

Anna Marie had picked a bouquet of daisies for the center piece while she was picking blueberries for the muffins. The green and white checked oil cloth with yellow flowers, which covered the table, was stretched out as far as it would reach. The white dishes and clear drinking glasses looked festive against the flowered oil cloth and the fresh flowers.

Almost as pretty as the tables we set for company back home, thought Marie.

"What's new around here?" Bootsy asked. "Is Tarpaper Annie still up the road? Did you do any more work on Slanty Shanty? Any bears around?"

"Now I don't want you kids hanging around up at Tarpaper Annie's. It's OK to go out for walks but you kids stay away from up there, you hear me," Mother said. "I don't want to have to remind you!" Her voice was firm and her brown eyes were flashing as she spoke. "OK?"

Tarpaper Annie's was a roadside beer joint about a mile down County Road 12 towards Ely. Sometimes the resort kids walked down there to buy pop or candy and to gawk at Tarpaper Annie. She was an unusual very colorful local character.

"Jack before you leave for Duluth, we need more minnows," Mother advised. "Maybe you kids want to go along for the ride?"

"You still drive up to Babbit, to Einar Maki's minnow place?" Al asked.

"Yep. Unless he delivers them down here. We usually load up a clean garbage can full once a week. His ponds are mucky, lots of dead trees along the edges. Kind of a spooky place. But his minnows are nice and fat!"

Anna Marie slipped away from the table. She went into her bedroom and returned wearing a red hardhat with a Soapbox Derby emblem on the front. She displayed the hardhat for the guests.

"Nice, huh? I got two of them. Don gave them to me," Anna announced. Don was Anna Marie's "friend" who had won the Soap Box derby in Duluth a few years earlier. "One is for me. One for Pat. We wore them to town. Lots of people stared at us but that's OK. Next week, I'm wearing a sailor's hat that Jean's boyfriend gave me. It's fun to be different, don't you think?"

Bootsy stared at her cousin. She was speechless. Jean rolled her eyes and snickered. The adults ignored the girl in the hardhat. They were talking. They had lots to talk over after a year's separation. Mother had only one sibling, Uncle Al, and her parents had been dead for years.

Uncle Al and Father planned a day of fishing at Bear Head Lake and a jaunt to their "secret" bass lake. If they had any luck there'd be fresh bass for Father to fry up with fried potatoes for breakfast. Only Uncle Al and Anna Marie liked fried fish for breakfast!

"You should have been up here last Tuesday," Mother said.

"Why?" Lizette asked.

"We had a terrific rain and wind storm. Came up quiet like. First, it was just muggy, so hot the air didn't move at all. Then, everything got quiet. There were no sounds of bugs or birds. The sky turned green then yellow. Very weird. The rain started to fall real hard. Then the wind came up. Oh my, what a wind! Trees bent and swayed. Leaves blew off the trees. It was awful. I had the kids check to see that the boats were up on shore and that the guests were in from the lake. The storm lasted a good two hours. Lots and lots of wind. Randy hid under the girls' bed. Dogs seem to know about storms. The blowing died down but it rained hard for hours. We made popcorn and went to bed early," Mother concluded.

"And the next day guess where we went?" Jean asked.

126

"Up the Echo Trail to scout out the trees," Anna Marie offered.

"Who cares about trees? There are lots of them all over," Bootsy stated.

"Shhh," Anna Marie warned through a glare.

Anna Marie knew full well how important that the big Norway pines along the edges of the Echo Trail were to Mother. Mother needed to see them herself, to check on them after the violent wind storm. So early that Wednesday morning, the girls made bologna and cheese sandwiches and packed fresh peaches and homemade peanut butter cookies to take up the Echo Trail for lunch. Mother made raspberry Kook Aid to take with in a large Thermos bottle. They loaded an old blanket, the food and a square black suitcase containing white enamel dishes, cups and silverware into Rosie. Their first stop had been in Ely where they picked up mail at the post office. Then they made very slow deliberate drive up the narrow gravel surface of the Echo Trail north of Ely, stopping to eat their picnic lunch on top of a huge boulder sitting along the road. There were only a few trees blown over by the storm. The exposed roots, clumps of dirt embedded in their tangle, seemed like prehistoric monsters to the girls. After a quick visit to the Lodge of the Whispering Pines (Mother loved the lodge's name; "so appropriate"), they headed back down the Trail to Buena Vista. Mother was quiet all the way home. Being a tree lover it made her sad to see the demise of those broken and twisted huge Norway pines toppled to the ground by a freakish summer storm.

"Don't peel the birch trees," was an admonition Mother used often around the resort even posting it in writing to remind the guests not to peel the bark from her precious birches. It seemed Mother felt that it was her duty to inspect the damaged trees lining a remote forest road. But the girls didn't mind the trip: They spent the day exploring the grounds of the other resort.

"More coffee anyone?" Mother asked standing in front of the stove holding the white and red enameled steel coffee pot in her hand. "No? OK then. Jack why don't you help Al and Lizette unload. Girls, time to do the dishes. Then you can swim. Lots of time to swim."

"You wash."

"No it's my turn to dry."

"Is not."

"Is too."

"OK, have your way, baby. Baby. Baby. Baby!"

"I'm not a baby," Anna Marie said through a pout.

"Are too," Jean announced.

"Hey stop that. You two draw straws or something," Father instructed, losing his patience.

"Supper around seven?" Mother asked.

"Supper? We just got up from the table," Father replied.

"You'll be hungry by then."

The sturdy oak table was always in the center of the cabin during meals. Otherwise it was tucked under the double casement windows out of the way. Mother insisted that the oilcloth covering be rolled up in a long cardboard tube and stored in the broom closet when not in use.

After the debate subsided Anna Marie swept the cabin floor and pushed the oak side chairs and long red pine bench back under the table. The red of the bench matched a red line painted on each end of the table.

"Think I'll pick some new flowers," Anna Marie announced when she'd finished her chores. "These look kind of droopy. Maybe I can find some brown-eyed Susan's or more daisies like these," she continued. "Wish we had a pretty vase, like at home. Oh well. A water glass will have to do."

The screen door banged behind the girl as she left the cabin. Inside it was quiet. Jean was curled up on her bed reading the Sunday comics. Randy was sleeping on the front stoop, his back against the porch railing. It was nap time for the dog after squeezing between noisy people's feet beneath the table. The other family members and guests were off doing chores or relaxing in lawn chairs pulled close to the dock to catch the cool breeze sweeping across the bay. A lone fly buzzed around a crumb of food someone had left on the seat of one of the chairs. All remained quiet around the resort until the next meal when there would once again be good food and noisy table talk; talk of fish that got away, talk of future plans and talk of ideas and perhaps the sharing of dreams.

Funny, Anna Marie thought as she searched for new flowers for the table, *how folks sitting around a table sharing a meal and their stories unknowingly share of themselves.*

TWENTY-ONE:
BIG SISTER

A skinny four year old girl sat on the curb, head in her hands, a sweater thrown over her narrow shoulders. She was waiting. It was November and a cold north wide scattered dry leaves down the sidewalk and whirled them up and away on frosty air. Jean peered anxiously down the street. She missed her mother and was tired of her aunt and grandfather fussing over her. At last a yellow taxi cab turned the corner and stopped in front of her.

Father had been present at the birth of his second daughter (not in the birthing room, of course, not back in the 1930's!) but at Mother's insistence he wasn't there to drive her home from the hospital. He was off deer hunting, a fact that would resurface time and time again over the years as a source of good-natured teasing.

The car door opened. The taxi driver quickly went around and opened the passenger door for Mother, who was holding a bundle wrapped snugly in a pink blanket. Jean eyed the bundle, which was making such a racket Jean placed her hands over her ears.

"Come look. Come see your new baby sister," Mother urged softly.

Jean walked slowly over to her mother's side and peeked quickly at the reddish puckered-up face of her bawling sister before stepping back, a determined look on her face.

"Give her back! Give her to the garbage man! I already promised him you would," Jean announced after meeting her sister on that blustery November day long past.

"Quick, Mother. Anna Marie's climbing out of her buggy!" Jean exclaimed breathlessly having run into the kitchen to share this latest report on her little sister.

By this time Anna Marie was a wiggly inquisitive nine-month-old who had managed to nearly escape her buggy. Mother looked at Jean with a smile. Jean sighed. It wasn't much fun keeping an eye on her baby sister, a sister who couldn't and wouldn't stay in one place very long. After Mother re-secured the baby, Jean sat on the lowest step of the front porch, one foot entwined in the buggy wheel, gently rocking the buggy back and forth. The large gray and black buggy was wrapped with mosquito netting. Jean peeked in from time to time, fearful that Anna Marie would wake up, bounce around and make that awful noise. Jean hated the crying. This noisy active creature had interrupted her peaceful world. After all, Jean was the oldest cousin and the only grandchild on her mother's side of the family. Now that was a family position to be reckoned with! What to do? Jean decided after a while that because Anna Marie was there for keeps she might as well give in and accept and love the new addition.

After all, Jean reasoned, *I am now the Big Sister.*

The telephone rang. It was a lazy summer afternoon.

"Your daughter is walking down the sidewalk with no clothes on," someone reported to Mother.

"Jean, I'll take the sidewalk in front. You go around the block and cross the street and check there," Mother instructed, dashing out the front door, the inside screen door banging behind her.

"Not again," grumbled Jean.

Anna Marie despised wearing starched cotton dresses and confining bonnets. She had no trouble losing the dress but, as she couldn't untie her shoes or a bonnet string, by the time she was captured, the bonnet would invariably be cockeyed, covering one eye but still firmly tied under her chubby chin.

The girls always shared a bedroom and a big mahogany four poster bed. Of course this also meant sharing toys and space.

One Christmas before Anna Marie was born Father and Grandfather Barber (Mother's father) built Jean a six room dollhouse out of wood salvaged from fruit crates. Over the years, the girls spent hours sitting on the floor or up on their knees playing with that dollhouse. When they had playmates over to play all the furniture and even the dollhouse dolls were divided into three piles. The six room house then became a tenement; each girl was allotted two rooms and a minimum of furniture.

There was a small room off the bedroom that became a playroom filled with dolls, bookcases and doll cradles. The girls often used the space to play library or office. They imagined their large clothes closet to be an elevator on the days they played department store.

After the resort was built in 1940 each June there was much discussion as to which toys, books and playthings to pack along to bring to Buena Vista. It was always a hard decision: What favorites to take, what things to leave behind in the quiet house for the entire summer!

At the resort Father decided to build a wooden platform as a secure and dry floor for a large canvas tent. He selected a spot that was already cleared beneath a tall pine tree near cabin one. The tent stayed up all summer and became a perfect playhouse for the girls on rainy days. Jean and Anna Marie would snuggle under old warm blankets reading books and listening to the patter of rain against canvas. The tent even had a small window ideal for peeking out to see who was approaching their sanctuary, to check on the weather or to keep open to catch the breeze on hot summer days.

In the 1940's "Let's Pretend" was a popular Saturday morning radio show for children. From ten until ten thirty when they were at home in Duluth the girls listened to the show intently each Saturday morning without fail. Both girls had vivid imaginations so pretending was always a major part of their play in the tent. They pretended they were a pioneer family living in the woods, queens in a castle or movie stars. The tent became whatever they wanted it to be. Imaginary food was created from pine cones, toadstools, clay, mud, pine needles and birch bark.

Tourists driving into the resort would pass by the tent and see a child's table and four chairs, all painted red and placed under an overshadowing pine. The table would be set with child-sized blue and white dishes, teddy bears and dolls sitting up properly, all ready for a make-believe tea party.

As the oldest of the cousins, Jean came up with brilliant ideas. She could also be very bossy. Anna Marie wasn't one to be compliant and she'd often resist her sister's demands and storm off to play alone. Gradually Anna Marie would find an excuse to check on the other kids, to see what was going on, to determine if they could exist without her.

The sisters shared chores at the resort when they grew older. Chores such as cleaning cabins, running errands, doing their laundry and driving into Ely for Mother. There were also chores to be done back home in Duluth over the fall, winter and spring. Chores were assigned that were fitting for a child's age. Most of the time, the girls worked well together, especially at the resort, where they would try to finish their chores in the morning, leaving their afternoons free.

Having a big sister to play with, work with, to talk to and argue with meant you were rarely lonely or alone. Jean taught Anna Marie and Anna's best friend Pat how to knit. Such patience and such a mess of tangled yarn amidst wails over dropped stitches!

The best time to talk with Jean was after supper when the girls were doing dishes.

"I did the cooking the girls can do the dishes," was a line that Mother was proud to expound.

It seemed like a fair deal.

During the school year the sisters shared their day doing the dishes at home. When they did dishes at the resort their conversation would center around plans for later, after the dishes were done, or for the next day. Mother would sit quietly in the background watching and listening to this special time unfold: sisters sharing things that make for a lifetime of memories.

Talk continued at home in the cozy confines of the big four poster bed. The girls would talk just before falling asleep. Well, they usually talked, that is unless they were angry with one another. It was again a special time for sharing, lying in that big bed, a pink and white chenille bedspread tucked in around them.

Of course during the school year, things were busy. Their house in Duluth had one bathroom and two girls rushing to get ready each morning. The mornings were noisy, confused, and sometimes tearful. At the resort mornings were less harried. There was no urgent time schedule to adhere to. But at home it was a different story.

"Hurry up and get out of there!" Anna Marie would shout at Jean who'd locked herself in the bathroom.

"I'll come out when I am good and ready," Jean would reply.

Anna Marie was the shouter. Jean was the door slammer. Both were trying to get ready in time for school. Mother's reaction? To turn up the white plastic kitchen radio, sip her coffee and ignore the whole thing.

The years slipped by. Doll buggies and toy dishes were packed away. Games, cards, water fights and sitting around talking with resort kids replaced the childhood toys during summers at Buena Vista. Most of the dolls ended up sitting in twin green painted wooden bookcases in the toy room of their Duluth home. There was one exception to this.

One spring day Jean and a friend, both in high school, were upstairs playing with dolls. The doorbell rang. Anna Marie answered. Two high school boys were standing at the door looking fairly uncomfortable.

"Is Jean home?" one of the boys asked.

"She's upstairs," Anna Marie answered, and then without thinking, she added: "She's playing with dolls."

The boys stared at each other.

Dolls?

"There are some boys down here to see you," Anna Marie hollered out.

The boys stayed on the porch. They were very quiet when Jean and her friend came down. And Jean, after learning what Anna Marie had revealed to the boys, was very very angry. Anna Marie knew it was mean. But she felt good about teasing her older and more sophisticated sister.

Later, Jean went off to college. Then marriage and work in the Twin Cities. Meanwhile, Anna Marie stayed busy. Her life became crowded with school, homework, dates, girlfriends and household chores. When Jean was at home, clothes and jewelry were borrowed back and forth, something made easy because they shared a bedroom. The night of Jean's wedding, Anna Marie crawled into that big four poster bed all alone. She felt lonely and abandoned. It was cold in that big empty bed that night as she cried herself to sleep.

Today, Big Sister Jean is still the eldest cousin. Anna Marie's and Jean's lives converge and flow with those of their children and their grandchildren. The resort years and all the years before and after have been shared in a unique way between loving sisters. Of course over the course of time there have been some harsh words shouted at each other and even a few times when they haven't spoken to each other for days.

What is it that binds people together? A sense of belonging? A sense of connection? A sense of family? Why do people choose to seek out one person, one sibling as a special friend? Anna Marie is convinced that the resort, with all its hard work, the play time, the fun time and the dull and ordinary time in between, strengthened her relationship with Jean.

The phone rings. Anna Marie answers it. It's Jean. After talking for a while the conversation slips back to earlier days.

"Hey, do you remember...?"

Off they go: Two grown women, talking faster and faster, laughing and maybe shedding a tear or two. Close to the heart and always, always sisters.

TWENTY-TWO:
END OF THE LINE-ALMOST

Chugga. Chugga, Chugga,

Rosie strained going up the hill from the parking lot near cabin one, down the winding gravel road, out onto Highway 21. Anna Marie gripped the steering wheel so tightly her knuckles turned white. She relaxed her shoulders, rolled down a window half-way and concentrated on driving. Mother was finally allowing her to take Rosie into town to run errands and pick up the mail. The old Chevrolet chugged along and ran smoothly once Anna shifted all the gears in proper sequence. She even remembered, as she drove towards town, to let out the clutch slowly just like Father taught her to do. After three miles the blacktopped road turned left, crossed the river emptying out of Bear Island Lake and headed east.

Anna Marie braked suddenly. A large doe stood in the middle of the road, head up, ears twitching, tail flicking slowly in watchfulness.

Hey there, missus deer, Anna Marie thought, *I'm on my way into town.*

She felt a bit silly talking to a deer if only inside her mind.

By the way. You're standing in the same spot where we used to catch the school bus. Yep, Jean and I went to school in Ely a couple of seasons-spring and fall-before going back to school in Duluth.

Anna Marie puzzled over the past.

Let's see. I had Miss Coffee, I think. And a Miss Ziegler. It was hard. Those Ely kids were smart. Jean had it even harder in the upper grades. I remember playing hopscotch out back of the school. The kids had drawn a hopscotch diagram into the dirt. It was all packed down hard, like a cement sidewalk. We were the first ones on the bus in the morning and the last ones off in the afternoon. Jean had to study every night. And we went to bed early. The days were long.

Anna Marie eased the car into gear as the deer wandered back into the brush. She glanced at the list lying on the plush seat next to her.

Stop at the community center with its gold leaf filigree ceiling to drop books off at the Ely Library. Go to Agnew's Ben

136

Franklin for shoelaces. Pick up groceries at Zup's. The bakery for bread. The resort laundry needed to be retrieved. And of course, she needed to stop and pick up the mail from the post office. It wasn't a long list but there were enough stops to keep her in Ely for two hours. It was Thursday, which meant hot bologna day at Zup's market. She'd find fresh limpa bread at the Finnish bakery. And, just as an aside, she'd check out the movies at the State and Ely theaters before buying a newspaper and heading back to the resort.

There were three roads leading in and out of Ely back then: Highways 1, 169, and 21. Greyhound buses departed daily as did the railroad, which hauled both iron ore and passengers. Seaplanes and bush pilots flew out of Ely into the border lakes of the United States and Canada.

It was mid-afternoon and quiet as she pulled into town. Men were at work. Women were generally at home doing housework. Kids being kids were off swimming or fishing or at play in the backyards of the homes in town.

Anna Marie parked in front of a neat brick building and hurried inside. She headed straight for Box 147 and quickly sorted through the mail to see if she'd received any letters.

Yes.

There was a thick letter from Pat, one from another friend named Shelley and one from Cousin Bootsy. She locked the box and left the post office. Back in the car she opened and read her mail. She smiled and swatted Pat's letter against the steering wheel.

Yes. Yes. She'll be here next week. Her mom agreed. She can come for a visit and stay two weeks, just in time for Roaring Stony Days and the carnival. And the Dick family will be here too. It will be perfect.

It was summertime; kids and fun! Oh sweet, sweet summertime!

Trips to town were always a joy. Once in awhile, Mother would rent a room at the Forest Hotel. It was only for a few hours, enough time for Mother to soak in a hot bath. Afterwards, once the girls were cleaned up as well they'd set their wet hair, tie scarves around their heads and have lunch at Vertin's Café.

Ah, the joys of living in the woods, Anna Marie thought as she drove past the hotel.

The streets were crowded with cars bearing out-of-state license plates, some hauling trailers and boats, many with canoes atop roof racks. There was a sense of excitement, of adventure you felt on the streets of Ely, a special town built on a hill only twelve miles from the Canadian border, a town surrounded by deep forests and clear blue sparkling lakes.

Anna Marie lamented that she didn't have the time to see Auntie Kay, Uncle Joe and her cousins, Lois, Donald and Janice. Joe would likely be at work underground in the Pioneer Mine. The family lived in Calumet Location. Uncle Joe grew a terrific vegetable garden and Auntie Kay grew fragrant delicately colored sweet peas against the back wall of their triplex.

Once when Anna Marie was staying with her aunt and uncle, the mine whistle blew and women came streaming out of the houses at the location, horror on their faces as the whistle screeched and screeched. An accident had happened in the mine but it must not have been too serious because everyone quietly returned home when no miners appeared. The women simply went back inside their homes and waited for their men to walk home after the shift. Anna knew something about the mines. Her father had once worked in the mines. She knew about the blasting, cutting, drilling and hauling of the iron ore, all done at the Pioneer underground. It was dangerous shift work, done by contract miners.

The clerk at the Troy Laundry was helpful, accompanying Anna Marie to the car with the bulky laundry bundles wrapped in brown paper.

"Let's see. Shoelaces-check. Laundry-check. Post office-check. Groceries-check."

Anna Marie glanced at her wristwatch. It was only three o'clock.; time enough to stop at the news stand next to the Ely Theater to pick up the newspaper and buy an ice cream cone. But not enough time to check at Vickie's Dress Shop or Penney's for new school clothes. That would have to wait.

Ely's two main thoroughfares Chapman Street and Sheridan Street lacked empty parking spots. She had to circle the block in Rosie several times before finding an empty spot and then rely on her meager skills to parallel park. It was tricky. A kind soul directed her from the curb helping her squeeze the car into a tight space. This was Ely, where folks were kind and always helpful, oftentimes displaying a sense of humor. Ely residents have to have a sense of humor. Each summer their town is invaded by tourists asking questions, needing help, most of them just plain confused. So many choices for camps, resorts and lodges. The Chamber of Commerce was active even back then and did an excellent job of assisting people in fulfilling their vacation dreams. Usually, the weather also cooperated and, throughout the summer, it seemed as if the town of Ely itself wore a smile.

"I've got time to stop and tell Janet that Pat's coming to town next week. I'll see if she can go to the carnival with us," Anna Marie said out loud though there was no one in the car to hear her as she pulled up to Janet Toms' house, parked and walked up to the front door. She banged on the door but no one answered.

I'll drop a card in the mail, Anna thought. *Gotta get these groceries home. Mother will be anxious.*

The next week, Anna Marie, Pat and the resort kids all piled into Rosie to go to the carnival in town. The carnival was part of Roaring Stony Days, a festival during which the town of Ely celebrated the coming of early pioneers to the town and surrounding area.

At the carnival Anna Marie poked her nose into a darkened canvas tent. Inside, seated at a cloth covered table, was a woman dressed as a gypsy. There was a crystal ball in the center of the table.

"Sit down miss. Show me your money."

"OK."

"Hmmm. I see trouble coming to you and sorrow. Maybe sickness. A tall dark handsome man will come to your aid..."

Outside the tent, the other kids wanted to know what the fortune teller had said.

"What'd she say?"

"Were you scared?"

"Come on, tell us!"

"Nope. It's none of your business," Anna replied.

"Well, OK for you! You sure are secretive. Must have told you something real bad."

"It's none of your business. Besides, I can't remember all the stuff she said. She was good though. She knew her stuff."

"Hah. That's a laugh."

"Let's go ride the ferris wheel."

"Can't. I get sick."

"Well, then you can watch."

After a full day at the carnival, the grubby, dirty, tired band of revelers headed back to the resort. Anna Marie had a throbbing headache, the result of too much going round and round, too many bright lights and noise. But even through her headache, she could remember the gypsy woman's words.

Back at the resort, sprawled out across the double bed, Anna Marie and her best friend, Pat, were talking.

"Say, do you think your parents would let our gang stay at the resort for a weekend in the fall?"

"Dunno. I can ask before you leave to go back home. That would be fun. We could stay in one cabin, drive into Ely and eat and eat. Almost like our pajama parties back home."

Sure enough, in October of that year eight giggling teenage girls and Anna Marie's parents headed north from Duluth to the Buena Vista for a weekend retreat. That time of year there wasn't much sun and some of the leaves were gone but cabin one was warmed by friendship and the heat of a coal briquette fire. Lois, Donna, Joanie, two Pats, Carol, Shelley and Anna Marie made up the crew.

Eight teenaged girls wearing warm flannel pajamas and nightgowns sat around the cabin on Friday evening eating hamburgers and potato chips. Anna Marie was the chief cook, the other girls, the bottle washers! There were loads of dishes to be done but it was fun when all pitched in to help. By the time the dishes were stacked and dry, it was dark outside but cozy and warm inside the cabin and a feeling of closeness prevailed.

"You should have been here last summer, all of you. We had so much fun," Anna Marie said. "Ely is busy in the summer. So many nice people working in the stores. The tourists are nice too. Not to mention that there are lots of great guys to look at!"

Anna Marie's friends were paying attention as she spoke.

"Don't you ever get bored up here all summer?"

"Where in the heck is Ely, anyway?"

Anna Marie was asked these questions, and many more, over the course of the weekend. As to the question about being bored, she always answered "no". How could you be bored? There were movies to see, library books to read, fish waiting to be caught, sunshine to be absorbed, clean, pine scented air to inhale and new people to meet. The time at the resort flew by.

"Well anyhow", Anna Marie said through a wide grin, "we went to the Roaring Stony Parade and get this..."

Rat-a-tat-tat. Rat-a-tat-tat. Rat-a-tat-tat.

She beat out a rhythm on the kitchen table.

"Pat, Jean, Bill, some of the resort kids and I were standing at the bottom of the hill waiting for the parade to begin but guess what? No majorette. It's not to be. But there was a guy in a black tuxedo stepping high and waving his arms in the air like a drum major. He was weaving back and forth across the street in front of the band, smiling to the crowd, doing a good job of marching in step if a little wobbly! And then Jean yells out 'Oh no. I know this guy. He's from Duluth. Turns out, he was in Ely for a morning wedding at the Catholic Church, St. Anthony's. As a member of the wedding party, he started celebrating a bit 'early'. He saw the band was all lined up, ready to go and they needed a leader. So off they went, the drunk at the head of the band, heads up, instruments flashing in the sunlight, stepping high. I heard he ended up out of money and sleeping in the church that night. What a celebration he must have had!"

Sunday morning found the girls tired and all decked out in the maroon and gold sweaters-Duluth Denfeld's school colors-and pleated skirts sitting in the front row of a small Ely church, attending service. After church Anna Marie drove the girls around town on a sightseeing tour of Ely and adjacent Shagawa Lake before heading back to the resort.

Only three roads lead into Ely. How you get there is up to you. Canada is a mere echo away. There are deep forests waiting to be explored. Walk quietly and explore. Just don't pick those trailing arbutus. Bend down and admire the flowers but please, don't pick them! Ely the end of the line? Not even close. It's the gateway to the Back of Beyond. Come visit, come laugh and live with the folks Up North for a while. You may leave, you may go back to your homes, your jobs, your town but you'll always return in body or in memory.

Ely, Minnesota the end of the line? Never. It's only the beginning. For Anna Marie. And for you.

TWENTY-THREE:
SO LONG FOR AWHILE

There was a thin river of gravel in front of Anna Marie winding its way through tall white birches. Her feet unconsciously followed the familiar trail. She knew where the path would lead her. Her mind was occupied by other thoughts. She wasn't thinking about the picnic supper that awaited her at the end of the gravel. This was the last time Anna Marie would see her friends at the resort that summer. This was to be her farewell to them. And to summer.

She walked with her head down, gently kicking dried grass and leaves ahead of her. The forest's vegetation had the look of late August. Goldenrod and Gentian Violets waved in the warm breeze. Anna Marie's heart was heavy, filled with a lonely, empty feeling as she struggled with what she would say. Such memories: Swimming until your lips turned blue; sun tanning on the dock; sharing secrets; and hours of building friendships, of simply spending time together.

She was too preoccupied with these thoughts to hear her friends call out to her as she approached the picnic table and campfire. But it was plain from their faces as she stepped into the light of the fire: Everyone realized that this was the last time they'd be together for quite awhile. Smiles appeared a bit too easily, an effort to cover up the undercurrent of sadness which infiltrated their minds as they thought of tomorrow.

The campfire burned brightly on the damp brown sand down by the lake, close to the water, the youngest of the group closest to its flames. Each kid held a stick skewering a sooty wiener, and with the care of great chefs, they turned the meat slowly over the fire cooking their wieners until the sides burst. Anna Marie sat down, virtually unnoticed, next to the fire to listen to conversations floating towards the water from the adults sitting at the picnic table. There was no laughter and yet, the faces shone with happiness. Over the course of a few days or a few weeks the resort and the North Woods had worked their magic. That time had given them a time to rest, to think, to play, to just be.

Across Bear Island Lake the late afternoon sun was setting behind trees bringing a close to the last day of summer. The juicy meat of sliced watermelon sitting on the table glowed red from the reflected fire. The kids gathered around the sweet fruit to finish the meal, and to drink cups of hot coffee, the pot cooked over the roaring flames of an open campfire.

Alone or in pairs, the adults soon left, seemingly giving in to the idea that summer nights belong to the young, to those who found it more difficult to say "goodbye". The noisy singing of the kids could be heard for an hour or more, in tune and out of tune, the only instrument accompanying them, a battered folk guitar. Some of the kids lay on their backs. Using logs as pillows, they stared up into the night sky once the sun was fully gone and counted falling stars. Others roasted marshmallows to golden perfection taking care not to have the sweet candy burst into flames at the end of their roasting sticks. The moon wasn't due to rise for hours but there was no rush. They had a fire, the starry, starry night and friendship. Shadows cast by the fire crept across their young faces. Their eyes, downcast and clearly sad revealed their thoughts. The voices suddenly stopped. It was starkly quiet save for one lone male voice, the strumming of the guitar, the story of a lonely cowboy being told in song.

Anna Marie could sense fall was near because a mist rose in soft swirls over the beach. In the distance, northern lights appeared and began to pulsate and flicker. It grew cold and she began to shiver. She moved closer to the fire, which, by then, was only glowing embers. She searched her mind for the proper words.

Goodbyes are always so sad, she thought. *Maybe it's better to say "So long for awhile"*.

The lone voice and guitar continued. The kids listened intently, their attentions captured by the spell of music and the chilling, beautiful night. Then one by one they silently left the dying fire and headed uphill to the cabins. Flashlights illumed the path. Fireflies appeared, darting this way and that against the night. No one said goodbye for they had read in each other's eyes the words they could not say. Saying "goodbye" to summer, to friends Anna Marie might never see again just didn't feel right. "So long for awhile" would have to do.

TWENTY-FOUR:
NOT FINISHED

It's been said that a journey once begun is never finished. Buena
Vista was sold in 1954 when Anna Marie was a junior in college.
There were many sleepless nights and countless anxious hours
spent by Mother and Father discussing the fate of the resort. Anna
Marie broke down and wept when the decision was finally made.
The North Woods had been such a part of her young life-her
journey. Fourteen years of towering pines, blue skies, whispering
birches, earthy smells, the odor of smoky campfires and sunsets so
glorious they could make you cry. She would never forget the
darkly mysterious, quiet nights when loons called across the lake
to each other as mist rose along the lakeshore like thin gray smoke.

Years later, long after the resort was sold and her life had
taken its course, Anna Marie was sitting at her kitchen table
sipping a cup of coffee. Her house was silent. It was so quiet; you
could hear the ticking of the grandfather clock in another room.
Outside the kitchen windows stately birches bowed with the wind
towards a stand of majestic pines. The woodsy setting in her own
yard reminded her of the resort.

Old photographs and one of Mother's old journals lay on
the table next to her empty coffee cup. One by one Anna Marie
picked up the pictures and studied them. The photographs had
been removed from old albums because Anna needed to add names
and dates to the back of each one. Mother's journal had a black
leather binding. The pages had yellowed over time. Leafing
through the journal, she found a short lovely poem written in her
mother's hand, author, unknown. She read the words aloud:

> *Life*
> *Each life is like a changing flower*
> *Like petals pale or colored free*
> *The years slip by drop*
> *Softly hour by hour*
> *And leave rich seeds of memory.*

Anna Marie wondered, as she took up her pen to write her own words, her own story, if the act of writing down what she remembered would mean that the journey was finally completed.

Never, she thought. *The journey will continue through the years, slowly, day by day. One memory will recall another, each memory precious, bittersweet, funny. Memories shared or kept private; memories of that special place, a place held close to my heart, the Back of Beyond.*

Non-Finita. Not Finished.

Acknowledgments

The question "Where in the world did you get the idea to write a memoir?" is one that I'm sure I'll be asked. Here's the answer to that question.

A few years ago, I was privileged to attend an adult education class "Indian Myths and Legends" taught by Duluthian Amelia LeGarde. As an assignment, Amelia asked us to write about a family legend. That's the impetus behind this memoir: A simple assignment to put pen to paper to preserve a family story.

In addition to Ms. Legarde, other teachers, teachers no longer with us, taught me to take pride in my writing. My fifth grade teacher, Mrs. Peterson asked me to read a Thanksgiving story I'd written in her class aloud to my classmates. What a proud moment! And then, in twelfth grade my Creative Writing teacher, Margaret Gatzweiler wrote the following words in my senior year book: "Keep on writing." So I did.

In the more recent past, members of the Monday Night Writers Group at the Duluth Depot assisted me in honing my prose through gentle criticism. I also benefited from cheerleading and editing by retired English teacher Lyn Homquist. Lyn helped turn early drafts of my stories into something whole, something worthy. Even folks who never laid eyes on my words helped, folks such as former *Duluth News Tribune* reporter Walter Eldot who admonished aspiring writers in our region to "write what you know".

More recently, friends and neighbors in the Two Harbors Library Memoir Group were kind enough to listen to my work, even asking me to read more! Such encouragement cannot be overstated.

Of course, I can't forget the friends, relatives and "resort kids" who created the memories reflected in this collection. A special "thank you" to my cousins Lizette (Bootsy), Jimmy and Johnny who, along with my friend Pat and my sister Jean made up the core group of the Slanty Shanty "gang".

I must also heap love and appreciation upon my daughters Julie and Heidi and their supportive husbands Brad and Nick as well as their children (my grandchildren) Amanda, Meghan, Caleb, Joseph and Madeline for their quiet confidence and support.

My husband Wayne lovingly endured my reading and re-reading each and every word of this book (including multiple edits) aloud. He deserves special commendation for displaying such patience.

To my sister Barbara Jean I can only say I remain in awe of these stories, these remembrances of time, these reflections of familial love.

As this project approached completion, Christian, my great nephew and an aspiring writer was kind enough to share youthful knowledge with an older writer. In the same way, Rene', Christian's mother used her artistic talent to create a book cover that does these stories justice and makes this author proud. Her smiles were also a source of inspiration as we thumbed through family albums in search of photographs to be included in the book.

Finally I'd like to thank my nephew Mark; author, judge, editor, publisher, husband, father of four and friend for prodding me with periodic questions such as "Where's *that* manuscript?" His gentle nudging compelled me to bring this project to closure.

I hope you enjoyed reading my stories and sharing my memories. Now it's your turn to put pen to paper!

Susanne Kobe Schuler

December 3, 2006

About the Author

Susanne Kobe Schuler is a native Minnesotan. Born in Duluth, she spent summers in the Ely area at the resort described in this memoir. She is a graduate of the College of St. Scholastica and a retired educator. An avid and active community volunteer, Susanne is the mother of two adult daughters, grandmother of five lovely grandchildren and resides with her husband Wayne in a state game refuge west of Two Harbors, Minnesota. Deer browse on their property and birch trees sigh in the wind outside their kitchen door, constant memories of time spent Back of Beyond.

Author circa 1950, Back of Beyond

Other Books from CRP

The Legacy (ISBN 0972005080 (2nd Edition); Cloquet River Press; Author-Mark Munger)

Set against the backdrops of WWII Yugoslavia and present-day Minnesota, this debut novel combines elements of military history, romance, thriller, and mystery. Rated 3½ daggers out of 4 by *The Mystery Review Quarterly*.

Trade Paperback - $20.00 USA, $25.00 CAN

River Stories (ISBN 0972005013; Cloquet River Press; Author- Mark Munger)

A collection of essays describing life in northern Minnesota, with a strong emphasis on the out-of-doors, the rearing of children and the environment. A mixture of humor and thought-provoking prose gleaned from the author's columns in *The Hermantown Star*.

Trade Paperback - $15.00 USA, $20.00 CAN

Ordinary Lives (ISBN: 9780979217517 (2nd Edition); Cloquet River Press; Author-Mark Munger)

Creative fiction from one of northern Minnesota's newest writers, these stories touch upon all the elements of the human condition and leave the reader asking for more.

Trade Paperback - $20.00 USA, $25.00 CAN

Pigs, a Trial Lawyer's Story (ISBN 097200503x; Cloquet River Press; Author-Mark Munger)

A story of a young trial attorney, a giant corporation, marital infidelity, moral conflict and choices made, *Pigs* takes place against the backdrop of western Minnesota's beautiful Smokey Hills. Reviewers compare this tale with Grisham's best.

Trade Paperback - $20.00 USA, $25.00 CAN

Doc the Bunny and Other Short Tales (ISBN 0972005072; Cloquet River Press; Author-Mark Munger)

A sequel to *River Stories*, this book is packed with over three dozen humorous, touching and thought-provoking essays about life lived large in northeastern Minnesota. Munger demonstrates once again why he is fast becoming recognized as a regional writer of finely crafted fiction and creative non-fiction.

Trade Paperback-$15.00 USA, $20.00 CAN

Suomalaiset: People of the Marsh (ISBN 0972005064; Cloquet River Press; Author-Mark Munger)

A dockworker is found hanging from a rope in a city park. How is his death tied to the turbulence of the times? A masterful novel of compelling history and emotion, *Suomalaiset* has been hailed by reviewers as a "must read."

Trade Paperback- $20.00 USA, $25.00 CAN

Esther's Race (ISBN: 9780097200598; Cloquet River Press; Author-Mark Munger)

An African American registered nurse confronts her past, her race, and her religion in this contemporary story of love, loss, addiction, and recovery. A powerful testament to the strength of the human soul.

Trade Paperback-$20.00 USA, $25.00 CAN

Visit us at www.cloquetriverpress.com.
Order direct from our Estore at the website!